OVER *the* HILL *and* BETWEEN *the* SHEETS

OVER *the* HILL *and* BETWEEN *the* SHEETS

Sex, Love, and Lust in Middle Age

EDITED BY

Gail Belsky

SPRINGBOARD

NEW YORK   BOSTON

Springboard Press
Hachette Book Group USA
237 Park Avenue, New York, NY 10017
Visit our Web site at www.HachetteBookGroupUSA.com.

First Edition: July 2007

Springboard Press is an imprint of Grand Central Publishing. The Springboard name and logo are trademarks of Hachette Book Group USA.

Library of Congress Cataloging-in-Publication Data

Over the hill and between the sheets : sex, love, and lust in middle age / edited by Gail Belsky. — 1st ed.
    p. cm.
  ISBN-13: 978-0-446-58079-3
  ISBN-10: 0-446-58079-1
  1. Middle-aged persons—Psychology. 2. Middle-aged persons—Sexual behavior. 3. Middle-aged persons—Attitudes. I. Belsky, Gail.
  HQ1059.4.O84 2007
  306.7084'4—dc22
  2006035226

10 9 8 7 6 5 4 3 2 1

Design by Fearn Cutler de Vicq

PRINTED IN THE UNITED STATES OF AMERICA

To Julian,
my partner in change,
who gladly gave me my dream

Contents

Introduction

The idea for this book came innocently enough when a friend made a confession at dinner one night. He often said things to get a rise out of my husband and me . . . all right, just me. But as we lingered over mussels and fries, he blurted out something that took us all by surprise: He's hot for middle-aged women. Suddenly, he finds them—us?—to be incredibly alluring. (I assumed this included his wife, who was sitting right next to him, but that wasn't clear.) He even slows down at the school-bus stop to check out the moms, wondering, and I quote, "what their lives are like and what they're thinking about."

"You've got to be kidding," I said, laughing. I poked fun at him the rest of the night but couldn't get his admitted proclivity out of my mind. The next time I was on the phone with a man other than my husband I had to ask: Do middle-aged men really feel this way?

Absolutely, said author and essay contributor Cameron Stracher. His forty-something friends often talk about middle-aged women, or Yummy Mommies, as one of them likes to say.

Where had I been?

In a cave, apparently, along with many other middle-aged women who have never once thought of cruising barbershops or bus stations for interesting-looking dads.

I am the last person I'd expect to do a book on middle-aged intimacy. The public discussion of sex—mine or anyone else's—makes me squirm. (For more on this sentiment, see Satellite Sister and author Lian Dolan's essay; she sums up my feelings perfectly.) But I was so intrigued by the Yummy Mommy thing that I wanted to do this book almost immediately.

I figured there'd be a disconnect between how middle-aged men and women experience love and sexuality, and that a collection of essays from both would result in an amusing he said/she said dialogue. But in the process of talking to male and female writers I discovered that their stories are not disconnected at all—nor are they truly about sex. In the broadest sense, they are reflections of who we are and how we cope with midlife's ups and downs.

By this age we know that change is constant, and often unpredictable. Some changes hit like bricks: illness, infidelity, pregnancy, divorce, and head-spinning love. Others are subtle and creeping, the result of living four or more decades—we get bored, grow weary, wise up, take stock, change direction, seek answers. We wake up to find that our love lives, among other things, have mutated—for better or for worse, but not forever. And we accept that.

Last year my annual mammogram revealed an atypical growth. By the time they took it out and biopsied it, I had spent eight weeks waiting to hear that I didn't have cancer. Eight weeks of stress and virtually no sex. Fear and worry had made me so tense that I was literally untouchable. Ironic, because there had been a period in my marriage, not so long ago, when I was equally unavailable—out of anger then, not anxiety. (The details are different, but the emotions are similar to what writer Eric Bartels describes in his essay.) Then a year or so ago, and for no particular reason, the anger lifted and sex became fun and easy again.

First a subtle shift.

Then a brick.

I walked away from the surgery with a huge sense of relief (obviously) and an unwanted souvenir: a one-and-a-half-inch purple scar and puckering indent above my right nipple. It was an ugly intrusion, and if I were younger, if I didn't already have stretch marks, cellulite, wrinkles, and a scar near my collarbone from skin cancer surgery, I might have been devastated. Instead I was just depressed.

My breast, the source of so much pleasure over the years, was now nasty-looking and painful. The scar was a built-in reminder that many women my age are not as lucky as I had been—and that I might not be so lucky next time. There was nothing enjoyable about that breast now, as far as I was concerned. But my husband thought differently. He wasn't fazed by it. Wasn't repulsed or afraid to touch it. So eventually my breast became just my breast again . . . with one big nick and dent. And I moved on.

When change hit novelist Caroline Leavitt, it nearly killed. In her early forties, after giving birth to her first child, Leavitt became deathly ill with a rare blood-clotting disorder. It was months before she could hold her baby and even longer before she could sleep with her husband— or even think about sleeping with him, since the state of arousal would stimulate blood flow and might cause her to bleed to death. She went overnight from being the sexiest pregnant woman alive to a being a bloated, battle-scarred survivor. And still, she managed to find her way back. To sex. And health. And looking toward the future, however altered it might be.

Change delivered editor and writer Michael Corcoran from a nearly sexless second half. Married young, he and his wife had three kids before they were twenty-five, effectively killing any real desire for sex. They might have gone on like that forever—he was resigned to it, in fact—but one little move shook up everything.

More or less, better or worse, empty or full—in middle age, we just deal.

The essays in this collection are as varied as the lives

and experiences of the writers themselves. Sarah Mahoney discovers phone sex in wartime. Jacquelyn Mitchard finds love in a hammock with a younger man. Anne Burt loses a love child. Cameron Stracher tries to escape real life with an ill-fated weekend in Vegas. Ann Hood and her husband are torn apart by grief . . . and held together by passion.

They all strike a chord because they all reflect a universal truth: with age comes acceptance.

Defining middle age for the purposes of this book was tricky since, really, it is a stage more than a statistic. If I had taken the mathematical approach using the latest government life-expectancy figures, the male contributors would all be thirty-seven and the females would all be forty. If, however, I had used Freedictionary.com as my guide, they'd range in age from forty-five to sixty-five. And had I consulted Answers.com, which defines middle age as "the time of life between youth and old age," they'd be somewhere between forty and sixty. But I didn't need numbers to know that just as Stephan Wilkinson wasn't old when he became impotent at sixty, Marek Fuchs wasn't young when he had a vasectomy at thirty-six.

It used to be that we had few expectations of sex in middle age. Now, the bar is set pretty high. In popular culture today, midlife sex is hot, hot, hot—and women are getting as much as men. We've got the *Desperate Housewives*, who have never been desperate a day in their lives, and the *Sex and the City* girls, with their million-dollar shoes and their unbridled passion. These new icons are buff and beautiful—and the fact that they are played by buff, beautiful middle-aged actresses makes them somehow plausible. Most of us, however, neither look like that nor live like that.

In a recent study of adults forty-five and older, more than half of the respondents said they believe that "sexual activity is a critical part of a good relationship, and that a satisfying sexual relationship is an important factor affecting their quality of life." Well, who doesn't? The study *Sexuality at Midlife and Beyond: 2004 Update of Attitudes and Behaviors* reports that half of those who have regular partners said they have sex once a week or more. Good for them. But we all know that numbers rarely tell the whole truth—and that, sometimes, they out and out lie.

Part I

FOR BETTER OR FOR WORSE

SEX AND THE YOUNGER MAN
by Jacquelyn Mitchard

I loved my husband Dan. We were married when I was in my early twenties and he a bit older. At forty-three, he was diagnosed with end-stage cancer. But I continued to crave the touch of him—this strong, comic, stand-up Italian guy from the west side of Chicago—as he waned to a shade. Each time we made love, there was a special poignancy and power, because we both knew the last time would have to come soon. A month before Dan died, his pain overcame our love.

What followed Dan's death was nearly three years of monastic motherhood, interrupted only by a few rabbity encounters (including one in a lifeboat on the *Queen Elizabeth*, and I'm not making that up). A year of desultory dating followed as I looked for Mr. Better-Than-Nothing.

I felt as though my womanhood, if not my attractiveness, was utterly extinguished. The man who'd lit up my board was gone, and the board went dark. It looked like forever.

Given what came before it, the story of my meeting with an absolutely brilliant-looking young man in his thirties who unaccountably found the idea of marrying a woman in her forties (and all her children) deeply erotic is all the more remarkable. He called what he hoped to have with me "a dynasty," and his point of view was so exhilarating in a commitment-fearful world, well . . . I couldn't help but fall in love too.

As the poet said, everyone who couldn't hear the music thought the dancers were mad.

Our friends literally laid bets on whether it would last six weeks or six months.

But this is what really happened.

I met him just as I walked into my house from a run. Sweaty and bedraggled in my Texas Rangers ball cap and baggy bike shorts, I was dressed to impress no one, especially not the carpenter who was helping remodel a bedroom into an office.

Did I notice his eyes, the translucent blue of a good sapphire, his natural grace, his ripped shoulders under a paint-smeared T-shirt?

Of course I did; I was human.

But our handshake was businesslike, not electric.

And that was just how I wanted it.

Months before, I'd informed all my friends that I

was finished. Through. The blind dates, long-distance e-romances, rendezvous with recycled past beaux, and all other passionate connection with life-forms bearing the Y chromosome—excepting, of course, my three young sons—were over and done with. I'd learned some not-very-surprising news from my dull dates. A widow who'd crossed the critical age meridian (forty), was neither genetically engineered nor artificially tweaked to look like Susan Sarandon, and who had children under twelve exuded a sort of reverse pheromonal allure.

But that critical age bridge had rendered me balky, too. I was unable to look dewy-eyed while listening to a monologue on the subject of one man's entire existence from eighth grade forward. Not even for the sake of being adored would I put up with self-centered recitations about the glory days of college sports, amazing business achievements, a hard-won par at that day's golf match; stinginess; passive aggression; a compulsion to discuss the shortcomings of the crazy third wife—or worst of all, the sad tale of the young lovely who *(sob)* didn't return his affections. The few who weren't leery or narcissistic simply didn't do it for me.

My life as a person and mother would endure. My life as a woman below the neck was over. I was a woman alone and at her sexual peak, but I could have appetizer affairs that would not involve my three sons—who were lonely, too, for another kind of male attention. The fathers of their friends, who could at least throw a ball overhand, were gracious. It would have to do. There would be no new papa in the offing. My children were too precious to me to settle for less. *I* was too precious to me to settle for less. Longing for the experience of new love (and to thumb my nose at the men who didn't consider my children value added), I went far out onto the end of a limb and adopted a baby daughter.

So there!

Now the man who crossed the moat would have to be a man of parts indeed! He had a specific description: He had to be robust, emotionally and physically, enough for the long haul. He had to have a degree, a tool belt, a sense of adventure, the desire for a big family, and something to talk about other than himself. And yes, he would have to make me weak in the knees. Absolutely sick with passion. Nothing less.

Wistfully, I'd made up just such a man for my second novel, *The Most Wanted*. All my girlfriends who read about Charley Wilder fell in love with him. All of them were rueful about the fact that such a man didn't exist in nature.

And so I meditated. Exercised. Went to therapy. Kept hoping that yearning would be extinguished simply by time and lack of oxygen. "How long will it be," I asked my pal Mark one day, "before I stop wanting to howl at the moon?"

He sized me up with a sad smile. "That would be never, I think," he said.

I was working in my bedroom one late afternoon when I saw Chris the carpenter leaning in the door frame. My breath quickened. Oh, he was a doll. I could see why the interior decorator who'd referred Chris to me had set her cap firmly to snare him. By then, I'd realized he was too cute and alluring to be pals with me, so I was brief in asking him what he needed.

He shrugged those chiseled shoulders.

"Just to talk," he said. I sighed. He looked like an athlete, so I waited for him to recount, in numbing detail, that championship season when the Avengers beat the Huskies in double overtime. But he wanted to talk about landscaping. And Thomas Jefferson. About astronomy and the grammatical oddities of English as compared with Spanish. We talked about pyramids and computer programming, symphonies and swing dance, the "Marseilles" scene in *Casablanca* and Chris's biological clock: He was (and remains) the only man I ever met who was worried he wouldn't marry soon enough to have as many children as he wanted. We talked for two hours.

By the end of the following day, I was weak in the knees. Sick with desire. Unable to eat.

I gave Chris an early copy of my not yet published novel to read. I was secretly hoping that he couldn't read and was for this reason doing remodeling instead of putting his degree in studio arts to a more profound use. However, he read the book overnight and told me the next day that the character named Charley reminded him of . . . him. Our chats grew longer. We ate lunch together and took rides after work, driving around in his crummy yellow van, singing old Tom Petty songs at the tops of our lungs, sitting on the hood and drinking champagne from paper cups, playing connect-the-dots with the stars. Chris's voice on the answering machine gave me goose bumps. I made up excuses (urgent remodeling issues) to call him back. One day as we sat talking on the porch, he took my hand. "I'm not making a pass," he said. "I just wanted to see how your hand felt in mine." I almost crawled up onto the roof. I felt as though I were sixteen again, cruising with the cutest boy in class.

It was great and time-limited. I told myself that was part of the allure. So I let Chris play basketball with the boys, and, in my faded jeans and my flannel shirt with the sleeves rolled up, I joined in, feeling as sexy as someone cavorting on the cover of a magazine. Nothing about it was serious, so nothing about it could hurt me.

Soon, Chris would be gone. He had a white-collar job lined up in New Mexico and was keen on relocating. My remodeling work would be his last job. Not once during all those three-hour lunch breaks did we even kiss.

"I think he's flirting with you," my assistant told me one night. "I think you should date him."

"I think I should adopt him," I said. "We're just friends. He's a child."

But he wasn't a child. Though he looked younger, he was thirty-two, little more than a decade younger than I.

He was smart and capable. He was a carpenter because he liked it and didn't care what anyone thought of that. He'd had a couple of enduring relationships but never lived with a woman. In one sense, that was good. A bond had never failed him. In another sense, it was awful: He'd expect every day (probably with the interior decorator) to be Valentine's Day. I had children. I couldn't be a doting bride. Bride? I was a nun! When I began thinking this way about Chris, I scolded myself. Everything about him and me as more than friends was ridiculous. Altogether. Especially the age difference, which might seem fairly trivial in this narrow moment of time but would yawn widely later on.

But I was so smitten that I finally rationalized I could risk . . . an appetizer.

So I asked him out for coffee. And when I dropped him off, I leaned over and kissed him well and truly. And it was he who pulled away.

"What's wrong?" I cried, sure he was thinking, Here's a middle-aged crazy who's mistaken a little friendship for attraction.

"I just don't like things that end," he told me. My eyes filled with tears. I wanted to grab him and hold on tight. I wanted to push him off an overpass. I'd taken an emotional protractor and drawn a careful circle around my heart. Did I want it breached?

"Go to New Mexico," I told him, "I'll find someone else to finish the job."

"Let's have dinner instead and talk about it, because I

don't think you know what I mean," he suggested. "You do eat, don't you?"

Not so much anymore, I thought, having dropped a size in two weeks. But we had dinner that night, a Friday.

Afterward, we went to Chris's tiny apartment. He'd locked himself out, and so he leaped up, grabbed the balcony rail with one arm, swung himself over, and opened the patio slider. I was positively woozy with lust. He came downstairs and opened the door. Everything was scrupulously neat and spare, except that he—like Charley Wilder in my novel—had strung across his living room an eighteen-foot hammock from the Yucatan. In a gesture both touching and telling, he showed me his photo album: his parents, including his mother who had married and given birth to him and his brother before she was twenty; his sister, from his father's second marriage, who was, at the time, *five* years old; and all the girls he'd loved before. Each of them looked as though she'd just finished her shift at Hooters. (Much later, a friend, commenting on one of those pictures, remarked what a beauty one of them was, adding kindly that she was probably as dumb as a post. She was a pediatrician, I admitted with a sigh. My friend asked, in honest befuddlement, "What was he looking for?")

He was looking, evidently, for me.

I thought we'd tumble into the hammock for a cheerful hour or so, but Chris wanted to sit on the terrace and smoke a cigar his stepfather had given him. An addiction! I thought gratefully. A way out! But he told me that he

smoked perhaps one a year. After smoking it and brush-
ing his teeth, he came back outside. We sat together in the
dark against the wall that had been baked warm by the
day's sun.

"You're a man of few words," I told him. "You tend
not to speak in whole sentences."

"I'm in love with you," he said. "That's a sentence."

I was dumbstruck.

Then I said, "Come on. You're a kid. You have all
these Robert Palmer girls in your photo album. Don't play
silly games. Or better yet, do play silly games. But not for
keeps."

"I always play for keeps," Chris said.

We undressed carefully. I took a long time folding my
clothes and modestly putting on the long T-shirt he'd given
me.

Chris, who's never told a lie, later revealed that he was
as worried as I was. I'd told him I had a cesarean scar as
big as the Rio Grande, and he was honestly concerned that
sex with an older woman might not "work out," that he
might miss the effortless bounce of younger flesh. I was
worried, terribly worried, about the same thing. Gravity
and childbirth had not been pals to my breasts or my behind, though I was as fit as I reasonably could be given the
demands of being an around-the-clock parent and wage
earner. Still, when we finally fell into each other's bodies (after exchanging results of our HIV tests), Chris said
aloud he hoped that I would get pregnant, because it would

solve a whole slew of other things. I didn't know what he meant, and I don't know if the earth moved. But the hammock nearly came out of the wall. And the board I thought would never light up again blew all its fuses. People say of sex that it's the most fun they've ever had lying down. This was the most fun I'd ever had horizontal or vertical.

"You're like a poem that gets up and walks around," I told him.

"You have the softest skin," he said.

"But am I beautiful to you? Is it like it was with younger women?"

"The truth?" he asked.

"The truth," I told him, biting my lip. "How do you feel?"

"Relieved," he said. "Relieved because yes, it was different, but it was different in a good way. I like that you're experienced. I like that your body shows that. I like feeling that there's a mind inside the body. You're a woman of endless possibility," he said, "in bed and out."

We spent the night in bouts of talk and urgent replays of the original act. I knew that I'd have trouble walking in the morning, but I told myself I was front-loading this pleasure, since it might be a long time before I felt such heat again. But when it was nearly morning, Chris said suddenly, "I thought . . ."

"You thought . . ."

"I thought you might . . ."

"Might what?" I prompted him.

"Do me the honor of marrying me," he said, and swallowed hard.

I thought, He's hallucinating.

But I shouted, "Yes!" without thinking.

And then, when I'd recovered and begun thinking, I wanted to recant. I asked, "What about the age difference? What about when I'm sixty and you're only pushing fifty? What about New Mexico? What about the children? What about the fact that I don't even know you?"

"As long as we talk all of it out, every step of the way, it'll be okay," Chris said, with a Zen calm that was deep but, I was to learn, only occasional. "And I always thought I'd marry an older woman with children and then have more."

"More?" I squeaked.

"And so this wedding . . ." he said.

"Everyone will try to talk us out of it," I told him. "My father. Your father. My brother. Your brother. My friends. Your friends. We'd have to fight people off. People will be laying bets on whether it will last six weeks or six months."

"What day is it?" Chris asked.

"It's . . . well, it's Sunday now."

"Okay. Do they do weddings on Monday?" he asked. "I've never done this before."

"I thought you didn't rush into things," I said.

"Who's rushing?" he asked. "I found the woman I want to marry. I'm not going to wait until you talk yourself out of it."

We ended up waiting.

Until Wednesday.

I would love to tell you that Chris and I have spent the past seven years in a beatific recapitulation of that first night.

In fact, we almost didn't make our first anniversary. We'd married in the middle, unlike most newlyweds, and never had the luxury of long, delectable days to explore each other's bodies and hearts. When someone mistook Chris for my younger brother, I refused to speak to *Chris* for three days. When an old boyfriend and I spent an hour on the phone, Chris sulked away a Sunday. I was a veteran parent, used to steering the ship. Single for nearly five years, I'd forgotten how much sheer breath a man took up in a house. Chris was a raw rookie, accustomed to the footloose schedule of a long bachelorhood. My insecurities and his inexperience nearly overwhelmed us. Those fine-boned Danish good looks drew stares from other women. Chris wondered why I spent time e-mailing other authors who were men.

Time, however, sealed us.

Eight months after we married, Chris adopted my children.

Nine months and two miscarriages later, we adopted our daughter, Mia.

Three years after that, through marvels of modern technology, we had a baby son.

Once, in the heat of battle, Chris told me, "You might

want to leave me, but you can't. I'm a reformed narcissist, and you're responsible for that!"

Gradually, it became clear that my sons accepted Chris. In fact, my youngest boy, just three when his father died, knew no other Dad but this one, though my eldest son, already thirteen when we married, gave Chris the run of his life before grudgingly giving in to the power of his gentle presence.

It began to annoy me when strangers, learning I had a much younger husband, assumed he'd married me for power or because I knew some arcane European tricks of sensuality. "You go, girl!" they marveled when they met Chris, and I fumed. His family gave him some grief for opting to be a dad at home whose wife "wore the pants."

Still, as years passed, Chris looked less like a boy model and more like a young father; and I, by dint of a little Botox and a lot of walking mingled with the tonic of joy, looked younger than I had when we met. We blended into a comfortable middle ground; the age issue melted, and we were able to tell the kids, when in doubt, stick it out. In our hardest times, I have never felt less than graced by having practically stumbled across a man with a gift for fatherhood.

And passion? Well, passion sometimes has to give way to exhaustion, midnight colic and early-morning spelling drills, nights at the emergency room and days in the grocery aisle. After a few months, we settled into the routine so common among parents: hiring a sitter and having a Saturday-night date in our bedroom.

But when we get the chance to be away together, even for a day, things between us are combustible. And the lights on my board that went dark so many years ago gleam again—sometimes filling the whole sky with sparks.

TILL FAITH DO US PART
by Ann Hood

When I met my husband-to-be Lorne I used to walk every Saturday morning from my apartment in the West Village in New York City up Hudson Street to St. Luke's Church, where I helped cook meals for people with AIDS. This was in 1992, and my neighborhood, near Christopher Street, with its condom shops and gay bars with blackened windows, was especially ravaged by the disease. It was common to see young men whose faces had splotches of red and purple leaning heavily on canes or walkers as they made their slow way down the block.

I never actually set foot in that church. Instead, I walked through a gate, past a garden that bloomed bright in warm weather, and into the kitchen. I am Italian American, raised with the philosophy that feeding people nourishes their souls as well as their stomachs. Someone else plated the potatoes au gratin and crème brûlées; someone else sliced the leg of lamb marinated in yogurt and spices; someone else set the tables and served the food and cleaned up afterward. Me, I cooked. And by cooking those few hours, I nourished my own soul as well.

By this time in my life, I had dabbled in and explored just about everything spiritual. When I ruptured my Achilles tendon hiking when I was twenty-two, I wrote *Buddhist* on the emergency room form under RELIGION. I puzzled over the silence and simplicity of Quaker meetings in the Berkshires one long lonely winter there. I lit seder candles and ate challah bread on Friday nights during a relationship with a Jewish man and visited the Ethical Culture Society down the street from my apartment in Brooklyn. I read everyone from Saint Augustine to Lao-tzu to the Bhagwan Rashneesh, and finally, when I reached the age of thirty-five, newly divorced, moderately successful, my spirituality felt rich and large and comfortable.

In many ways, by the time I met Lorne, I had come full circle. My family's spirituality came from other people— helping them, sharing with them, talking to them, and, yes, feeding them. I grew up sitting around a kitchen table with a platter of spaghetti and meatballs in the center, a pot of coffee bubbling on the stove, and various generations of aunts, uncles, cousins, and friends filling every chair and corner of the room. At that table, I learned about love and loss, faraway places and broken hearts, strange diseases and miracle cures. As one of the youngest, I didn't say very much. I ate wine biscuits twisted into pretzel shapes and hard bread dipped into tomato sauce, tight batons of prosciutto and crunchy stalks of fennel dripping with olive oil. I ate and I listened and my soul and heart grew and expanded in that kitchen.

Ostensibly we were Catholic. But on snowy Sundays, or busy Sundays, or sometimes on any old Sunday, my grandmother climbed onto our kitchen table, threw holy water at us, and gave us special dispensation to stay home from church. Instead, I helped her mix the meat and spices for meatballs and got to eat them hot from the frying pan. In summer, we abandoned church altogether and spent Sundays from sunrise until dusk at a lake an hour from home. There, in the cold early morning, my father fried bacon and eggs in a cast-iron skillet over an open fire. When it got dark, we huddled together at campfires after dinners of barbecued chicken and marinated London broil, and desserts of marshmallows toasted on the long branches we had collected during the late afternoon.

When I was twelve, I abandoned Catholicism and churchgoing after the priest told me during confession that my entire family was going to hell because we spent summer Sundays together at the lake instead of attending Mass. Even then I understood that my spirituality came more from those long days swimming, hiking, and eating together than it did from sitting bored in an overheated church.

Although mutual lapsed Catholicism was one of the things we shared, Lorne had in fact been a more serious Catholic than I ever was. Various family members sang in the choir, and the kids all joined the youth group, playing guitars and taking ski trips and camping trips. While my parents looked relieved when I announced I was finished with church, Lorne continued attending Mass all the way through college and into adulthood.

I realized right away that Lorne was more religious than I. He had joined a Protestant church, and when his marriage was falling apart, he had gone to talk to his minister; when mine was on the rocks, I sought solace with friends and family. I didn't *have* a minister, of course. But Lorne did. He attended a big ornate Congregational church in Providence, where he joined various committees and ate at potluck suppers. When he drove, he got inspiration from tapes of famous sermons by renowned preachers. One summer, years earlier, when he was in graduate school, he worked for Church World Service, and he still counted the various ministers and Riverside Church administrators among his best friends. It seemed to me that church and spirituality were linked in Lorne's world, and separated in mine.

But when we fell in love that spring, it was fast and furious. The power and passion of that love made me believe that we could overcome everything: ex-spouses, political differences, the two hundred miles that lay between us. Spirituality—a private thing—and religious alliances and alienations seemed easier to work with than all of the other obstacles in our path. Besides, when kissing someone makes you swoon, makes your mind go blank, makes your stomach tumble, it feels at that moment like nothing else really matters.

That was why, in what felt like a minute, I left my beloved New York City behind to be with Lorne in Providence. Pregnant with our first child, Sam, I became a recalcitrant, though not entirely unhappy, member of that Congregational church. By the time I had our second baby, Grace, I was almost enjoying the social aspects the church offered. At the coffee hours and auctions and sing-alongs, I would spot another mom from Sam's preschool or the parents of a baby Grace's age. Taken out of my familiar single, childless world of Manhattan, I had to find new friends, new places to meet people, a new way of life. Church became one more way to navigate this new territory of wife and mother, one more connection in a marriage already solidly passionate and intimate.

Although sometimes I left church spiritually invigorated or intellectually challenged, more often I left simply happy to have watched Sam lead Grace hand in hand to children's hour or delighted at the sight of them in makeshift costumes during the Christmas pageant. Even now, I can muster something like that spiritual bliss I felt back then when I imagine this tableau: my family—Lorne, Sam, Grace, and I—dressed in our Sunday best, Sam's shirt untucked, Grace's hair snarled, my hand folded into my husband's, our bellies full of homemade waffles, the four of us entering that big yellow church with the sun streaming through its elaborate Tiffany windows.

Then the unthinkable happened. In April 2002, Grace, five years old, died suddenly from a virulent form of strep. The family life I had so carefully nurtured for a decade came to a grinding, confusing halt. Who does a mother turn to for blame and hate at a time like this? God, of course. For all the uncountable moments over these past ten years when I had paused to thank God, now I turned on Him. One sunny morning, just a few days before Grace died, I dropped her off at her kindergarten. It was uncharacteristically warm for April, and I swear the sunlight pouring from that bright blue sky looked positively golden spilling onto my station wagon as I watched Grace walk inside, her purple-spotted backpack bobbing, bouncing behind her. The sight of her and all that sunshine made me so grateful that I was overcome. I pulled over and thanked God for this day and these beautiful children.

When Grace died a few days later, my sense of betrayal was enormous. I told this story to our minister, a woman with two young children of her own. "It's so terrible," she kept saying over and over. But had I drawn attention to our good fortune that day in my car? Had I jinxed my family? I had read somewhere that Hmong babies wear elaborate hats that look like flowers from above, so that spirits flying past will mistake them for blossoms and leave them alone. Had my gratitude somehow tempted fate? But the minister could only shake her head and tell me how terribly sad it all was. Please, I told my friends who stood sentry by my door and telephones, please don't make me talk to her again.

Foolishly, I believed that other clergypeople might hold the answers I screamed to God for every night. I watched as my husband's seemingly unshakable faith wobbled too. Together, a unified force, we drove to talk to famous rabbis, priests, religious experts on loss. Dutifully, Lorne took notes, asked questions, listened. But I saw how their eyes drifted toward the clocks on their office walls, and when an hour passed, they assured us time would heal and sent us on our miserable way.

Still, Lorne took solace in these visits in a way that I could not. The only shard of comfort I could find was in friends' willingness to sit with me for endless hours and let me wail at God and the world. Lorne believed in a randomness in the world that I did not; I sought answers where he believed there were none.

Yet even in our grief, we made room for each other's spiritual differences. People fed us with aluminum pans of lasagna and fancy stuffed chicken and thick creamy soups; chocolate chip cookies and brownies; expensive wine and single-malt whiskey. But at night, in our three-legged house, we found comfort, as we always had, in each other's arms. Despite the long hours apart—Lorne at his office, me at home with friends—in our bed, our old passion helped us get through until morning. The powerful connection that had brought us together remained, amazingly unchanged. More often than not, crying became part of our lovemaking. Our bed, into which Sam and Grace had so happily tumbled each morning, where we all had squeezed together to watch movies, now held our grief and our fragile selves together.

That summer, when I was teaching writing at the Chautauqua Institution in upstate New York, the minister there gave a series of morning sermons on the landscape of grief. His own wife had died young, and that loss sent him on a spiritual journey away from the familiar church and city he had known. Changing from minister to teacher, moving from Nashville to Indianapolis, traveling to far-flung places, had all been part of his journey of grief. When the sermon ended, I made an appointment to talk with him.

That afternoon, in the hot study of the Victorian house where he stayed, I told him about losing Grace. I told him how ministers and priests and rabbis had been able to offer only platitudes, instead of answers, or even comfort. Then I said out loud the horrible thing that I had been thinking for months now. "I don't believe in God anymore," I said. Dan nodded. He understood. It's difficult to believe in something that doesn't make sense anymore, he told me.

When he stood, I realized my hour was up. Although I knew he wouldn't make hollow promises about time healing as he ushered me to the door, I still felt the familiar anger rising in me. Who had taught these religious people, I wondered, that a mother's heart could be healed in sixty minutes? But Dan surprised me. "Well," he said, "you're stuck with me now. Here's my e-mail address, my home phone, my cell phone. Contact me any time. Day or night."

Surprised and grateful, I left that room feeling spiritually validated. I could hate God. I could not believe in Him at all. Why should I put myself through the motions of going to church when I felt betrayed by it? There were so many things I had stopped doing to avoid the horrible pain they brought. I never drove down the tree-lined street where Grace's school sat or the block behind Brown University where she had taken ballet class. When I passed the Children's Hospital, where she died, I kept my eyes focused on the highway ahead, never glancing to my right. I didn't go to Old Navy or open the Hanna Andersson catalogs that seemed to slide through my mail slot with alarming frequency. If I could avoid all of this, then why would I go to church ever again?

No sooner had that first autumn without Grace arrived, with its onslaught of back-to-school clothes and lunch boxes and promise, than Grace's birthday came. I drank too much rosé and ate her favorite foods of sliced cucumbers and shells with butter and Parmesan. Birthdays, back to school, and the horrible promise of Thanksgiving and Christmas right around the corner. How was I going to get through it all?

Then, one Sunday morning, Lorne said he wanted us all to go to church. I wanted to flat-out refuse. But so desperate was I for help, so desperate to make our little broken family whole again, that I went despite my discomfort. As we slid into our usual pew, a family of three, now, instead of four, I felt everyone's pity pouring over us. It wasn't pity that I wanted, or even sympathy. I wanted Grace back. And short of that, I wanted God or someone to help me understand why she was gone and what to do without her. Sam squeezed my hand. "I want to go home," he whispered. I glanced at him and saw his cheeks were wet with tears. When it was time for children's hour, I watched as all the same pairs and trios of siblings skipped down the aisles together, hair ribbons dangling, shoelaces untied. Sam was weeping now, unable to control himself. We all were. The minister's words about kindness and fellowship sounded hollow. I couldn't wait to get out of there. I never wanted to go back.

But Lorne, in that openhearted way of his, found solace in the sympathy of the congregation and comfort in the minister's sermon. All those years ago, our different and varying views on spirituality had seemed interesting and manageable. Now we stood on opposite sides of a spiritual divide. Lorne still believed in the Christian tenets that had helped him through his lifetime; I once again found myself questioning them, unbelieving, alone. We debated our different opinions and needs until, with no truce in sight, we turned silent.

Over the next months, I vacillated between gritting my teeth and accompanying Lorne to church, where I often walked out over some philosophical disagreement or simple frustration with the banality of the service, and digging in my heels and refusing to go. "It makes me too sad," I explained. "It makes me sad too," Lorne said. Still, somehow, being there did help him in his grief, and it only made me angrier. On the mornings I stayed behind, I drove the fifteen miles to my mother's house and let her make me a big breakfast of bacon and eggs and toast and coffee. I found much more comfort in an hour there than I did at church.

I remembered how during my years of visiting different religious places, I had enjoyed the Sunday mornings I spent at a Unitarian church. When I'd first moved to Providence, I had gone alone to one right up the street from our house, and found it more appealing than the Congregational church we attended. But Lorne preferred ours and didn't like that Unitarians weren't Christians. Since it mattered more to him than it did to me, I let it go. But now I wondered if some spiritual compromise was necessary. We made an appointment to meet with the minister of our church to see if she had any ideas about our spiritual differences.

In her high-ceilinged office, she told us about other married congregants who didn't come to church together. Some went to separate churches. Others had one spouse who didn't go to church at all. I tried explaining how church—this church, in particular—made me feel. How seeing children Grace's age there opened my grief all over again; how the shadow of her in the pageant, emerging from church school, holding Sam's hand on the way to children's hour, all of it, made me want to run out of there screaming. "It sounds like you shouldn't come then," she said, and although her advice held both logic and compassion, I once again felt let down. Ultimately, my spirituality was between me and me. Yet I felt torn in different directions. Shouldn't someone in charge help me straighten these feelings out?

Together in that office, Lorne and I came up with a plan to try other churches once a month. Since we only went to church a couple of times a month anyway, this left me with only one Sunday to have to face my demons here. The next week, we all went to a Baptist church with an African American congregation. The minister's sermon was powerful, and the experience satisfying. Then the holidays came; I left for teaching out of town; we went away; and before I knew it we were back to the old Sunday struggle, our decision to visit other places once a month abandoned. In some ways, I dropped the ball on finding these alternative religious experiences. Grief had worn me down; it had exhausted me. My desire to read the religion section of the newspaper to find interesting sermons, unusual services, different congregations, flagged. Deep down I knew this idea was just a stalling technique. I wasn't going to join the alternative church that met in a real church's basement; I wasn't going to return to my Catholic roots; I didn't want to become Episcopalian, Zen Buddhist, or a practitioner of TM. I just wanted to be angry at God.

I began to wonder what I would have done had I been my younger self, instead of this forty-seven-year-old woman. When I was in a relationship with a practicing Jew, I had given him free rein: no Christmas tree, no Easter eggs. Instead, his contemporary silver-crafted menorah held center stage on our shelf of treasures. Although it could be argued that my own beliefs were subjugated to his, an error women who are far away from middle age often make, in truth I felt comfortable enough with my spirituality to keep it to myself. I spent Christmas and Easter with my family, and he came along, happily joining in our home-made sangria and Christmas gifts. It was almost a relief not to drag a Christmas tree up to our fourth-floor walk-up. Since my own family didn't attend church, I never felt that I gave up that much.

But now I had a child to consider, a broken heart, a churchgoing husband, and I didn't believe in God. In many things, middle age has allowed me to easily admit defeat. I no longer feel like I have to do a difficult hike because everyone else is doing it, or that I must keep up shallow friendships, or that I have to read a book I don't like all the way to the end. That same maturity that allowed me to prioritize all kinds of things now made me more confused. In a moment of clarity, I agreed to go back to church.

It was another September, and I harbored a small hope that in church that Sunday I would find strength to face what had slayed me last year: back-to-school and Grace's birthday. I felt good seeing how this simple decision to go with him without an argument made my husband so happy. What was two hours a month after what we had been through?

We settled into our pew, and as the choir began to raise their voices, I skimmed through the program. As an overachiever, I always like to know ahead of time what the Bible verses are going to be so I can read them before they're read out loud, and I like to mark the hymns that are going to be sung. That was when I saw that coming up, soon, was "Amazing Grace." When you have named your daughter Grace and she is alive and thriving, it is exciting to see her name in books as the snappy protagonist or on the sides of pharmaceuticals or even in this most beautiful hymn. But everyone in that church, including the people who chose that song, knew two things: Grace's birthday was that week, and that song had been sung at her funeral, achingly beautifully, by my sister-in-law.

Already, prayers had been spoken and other songs had been sung. At any moment the organ would play those heartbreaking opening chords. I grabbed my coat and walked out of the pew, down that center aisle, and out the door, where I sat on a cold stone bench and cried like I might never stop. When I felt an arm slip around my shoulders, I expected it to be one of the ministers or other laypeople who help out during the service. But it was my stalwart friend Amy, who had sat and held my hand, took me out for teary dinners, taught me how to cast off when I learned to knit in those dark new days of grieving.

"I saw what was on that program and I couldn't believe it," Amy said. "Then I saw you walk out."

Amy sat with me in the sharp autumn sun and let me cry and rant against church and God, while Lorne remained inside. I wondered how he could do it, how he could sit there and let that song wash over him. Was he stronger than I? Or was this just another example of our different ways through grief?

We made another meeting with our ministers. "How could you?" I asked them. "You knew how hard it is for me to walk in here, and then you play that song." I explained that as a popular and beautiful hymn, it should be played. But so close to Grace's birthday? And without any warning? Even if that didn't occur to anyone, we were always getting calls to come to meetings or to ask us to bake cookies or work on a sandwich brigade for the homeless shelter, but no one could call us to apologize after they saw me walk out in tears?

It *was* a mistake. They were sorry. It would never happen again. In fact, they would not play "Amazing Grace" in September, or in April, the month Grace died. I looked into the faces of these people—people no closer to God than I was—and saw their fear. Both of them had young children. If I had lost Grace, anything could happen. Was that why it was so difficult for them to offer comfort, to help me come up with answers, to massage my wounded spirit?

In the gumbo of spirituality, of church and religion and God and beliefs and faith, it is hard to separate one from the other. It has been three years since Grace died. My husband has turned fifty since then. He is a handsome man, but sorrow has taken some of the twinkle from his eyes. He is a man who believes in the power of church and religion. He wants a simple thing: for his wife and his son to stand beside him and lift their voices in a song of gratitude for what we have and for having had Grace at all. I try to give him this. It isn't easy, but I am trying.

I see now that my own journey has led me back to what I knew as a child facing down a priest who was hidden by the screen of the confessional; what I knew as a younger woman living alone in New York City, chopping basil and peeling potatoes for the dying men in my neighborhood.

Every evening I cook for my family. I spend too much money on a perfectly ripe cheese. I buy fancy crackers from Italy. I boil the water for spaghetti and carefully cook pancetta and garlic to make a carbonara. I toss this with the pasta, mix in eggs and good Parmesan cheese. Right before I serve it, I add two egg yolks. This is the secret to real spaghetti carbonara. I believe in this: good food, the sounds of forks against plates, the perfect blend of flavors. And later, in the night, I believe in the quiet sound of my son's deep breathing as he sleeps; I believe in my husband's hand, resting even in sleep on my breast, trusting, loving, there. Even now, there are still days so beautiful, I almost believe in God.

LEAVING LAS VEGAS
by Cameron Stracher

꒰꒱ Five in the morning, heart beating madly, I slip from the hotel room and make my way back to the airport to catch a plane for home. Las Vegas was a dream, a nightmare frenzy of alcohol, money, and beautiful women. It has made me sleepless with anxiety and fearful of the future. An insomniac cursed by rue and rumination.

It wasn't supposed to be this way. I left my house in suburban Connecticut for a weekend bacchanalia with my two oldest friends. As middle-aged dads firmly entrenched in our respective middle-life crises, we felt entitled to the respite, the break from the constant demands of work and domestic responsibilities. Vegas was where we would land and refuel, and woe to those who slowed us down.

But sixteen hours later I am boarding a plane, headed

for the same life I have just fled. The promises of freedom and the fountain of youth have not materialized, if they ever existed, and my search for them has been something both mysterious and mundane. Three hours later my friends will wake, and not understand. They will be worried, then confused. Where is Cam? What has happened? What is wrong with him?

I rewind the weekend, searching for the answers. When I met them at Bellagio, my friends were flush with liquor and cash, ready for anything. Peter, a television producer, had flown in from Los Angeles. David, a lawyer, came from Boston. Since we graduated high school, twenty-five years ago, their careers have ascended like fantastic birds while mine has swooped, dived, and drifted. Lately, I have struggled to pay the bills in a town where money is a second language. My third book has been rejected by every publisher in New York. I've taken to wandering the house at night like a zombie or vampire, undead and cold to the touch. The cure for my ills, my friends insisted, was Vegas.

Our first stop is a bank of slot machines where Peter feeds a machine cash like a boy nourishing ducks. His losses flash brightly across the screen: bar, bar, bell. Undaunted, he burns through his money in a matter of minutes. I count the bills, measuring the damage. Then, just as quickly, his luck turns, and he wins everything back and more. I tug at his sleeve.

"Let's go," I say. "Cash it in."

But he cannot stop. He wins with a steady mechanical progress, punching the buttons as if preprogrammed. Soon, he has lost his winnings again. He is about to pull the lever another time when I grab his arm and physically pull him away.

"I was winning," he says.

"Until you lost it all," I say.

"That was fun," he says, as if trying to convince me.

"Slots is a loser's game," says David. He is used to Peter's antics. The two of them bicker for a few minutes about who has lost the most over the years, each reminding the other of a staggering sum. They have been coming for nearly two decades, while I am a "Vegas virgin." David reassures me, however, I have nothing to fear. "You have to play to lose," he says.

In my wallet I have tucked away fifty dollars, which is about the most I can afford to waste. My friends have offered to pay my share of the hotel room, and I am both embarrassed and relieved by the offer, like a college student whose father gives him money to go to the movies. Now that we're here, however, I cannot bring myself to remind them of it.

Next stop is the spa, where the menu is pampering. We have massages and facials, and our bodies are scrubbed, buffed, and polished. Afterward, we sit in a hot tub like Roman emperors after a conquest.

"This is the life," says Peter.

The water is so hot it feels like we are ingredients for

soup. I imagine our skin sloughing off, the water turning viscous and yellow. I look down at my narrow chest, the sparse field of hair turning gray. My body has not aged well. Or, rather, it has as well as can be expected from a man who has spent two decades sitting at a desk, driving to work, raising children, eating breakfast over the sink. The time I had to work out, sleep late, eat properly, has vanished with my youth.

We make dinner plans. Nobu or Charlie Palmer's? Peter calls his assistant from his cell phone in the locker room, and she books us a table at nine. We shower and shave, then stroll back through the Bellagio, stopping at a bar for cocktails and a cigar. The activity has picked up, and all around us people are throwing away money. "It's a casino," says Peter, when I mention it.

Maybe he's right; maybe I've missed the point. I am not a gambler, even if I had the money to toss around. But the ease with which my friends enjoy themselves weighs on me, reminding me of how I live now and emphasizing our differences. David has dedicated himself to his legal career and succeeded at it, while Peter has followed a more creative path and has had similar accomplishments. My life, in contrast, seems stuck in a purgatory between vocation and avocation; by embracing neither, I have succeeded at neither.

The mild melancholia I have been nursing these past months seems suddenly virulent. The very cure threatens to send me on a downward spiral. I push away my thoughts, and force myself to focus on the conversation. The waitress brings us another round. She's thirty-nine, with an eighteen-year-old and an eight-year-old. She tells us she's been working in Vegas since she was twenty-one. Her ex-husband is a croupier. Her current boyfriend is in Miami. Peter takes her picture on his cell phone.

We leave the bar and stroll out into the casino. Groups of twenty-somethings prowl the floor like pack animals. Their skin gleams and teeth shine. The men are buff and ripped, and the women are fantastic creatures with impossible bosoms and legs that do not end. We cannot stop ourselves from staring. They do not look at us but walk right past, as if we are invisible or, worse, their fathers.

"How does a guy get some of that?" asks Peter.

"You have to pay for it," says David.

At dinner, we split a bottle of wine. We are sitting next to a table of young women, a bachelorette party. They shriek at every word, drawing our attention and interest. David orders a second bottle, and then a third. I wonder how much they cost. My buzz turns thick and unpleasant. It seems as if David is not talking *to* me so much as talking *at* me. The women's voices rise to a high pitch, piercing our own conversation, drowning us with sound.

We pay our staggering bill, stumbling as we leave the restaurant. "I want to do some gaming," David says.

We walk around until David finds a table he likes. He sits, and a waitress brings him a drink. Peter joins a different game and motions for me to come over. I watch for a while, switching between them, until I get bored. Then I wander across the floor.

Young couples crowd a roulette table. They roar as the ivory ball spins through its paces then groan when it falls onto an open number. They throw down more chips and laugh as if winning is the last thing on their minds. An attractive woman—a hooker, I realize—smiles at me. I turn away, suddenly self-conscious and embarrassed. Is it because a hooker is looking at me, or because the only woman who will look at me is a hooker? I am not sure. I am feeling old, and unattractive, and poor. I need to find my friends.

David is where I left him. He can barely keep his head above the table. Even the dealer, a diminutive Korean woman, looks concerned. He splits a pair of fives, then loses both hands. There is a pretty decent-sized stack of chips in front of him, but he can't remember whether it's his original stake or whether he bought more. The dealer tells me I should take him home. "He no good," she says, and I agree. Peter joins me, and we stand him up. It's time for bed, I say. Tomorrow's another day. We head for the elevators, weaving our way through the stoned, buzzed, and smashed.

Back in our room, I go to the bathroom where I take two Ambiens and brush my teeth. I tell my friends I am going to sleep. They seem offended and argue with me about staying up, even though they both look as if they may pass out at any moment. " 'S Vegas," says David, as if that explains everything. "Good night," I say. I am out like a light.

Somewhere in the middle of the night I awake. The room is bathed in an eerie blue glow, and I can hear the sound of soft moaning. I realize the television is still on. I shut it off, then sit on the edge of my bed. I feel dizzy and woozy, but cannot fall back asleep. David is snoring, and Peter sleeps with one arm across his face, the way my son did when he was a little boy.

If I just sit for a while, I tell myself, I will remember why I am here, although I am not a card player, not really a drinker, not a frequenter of whores. I will remember what I am escaping, and why I believed Vegas offered the cure. I will picture the comfort of strangers and the consolation offered by good friends. But instead I think of the expensive meals we will eat tomorrow, the gambling we will do, the conversations interrupted by background noise and distraction. I imagine how I will feel when another young woman looks past me, when my own body revolts me, when my career seems paltry, foolish, and ill-advised. Each step through the plastic palace mocks me, calls my choices unworthy, fills me with remorse.

I am seized then by an unexpected longing: not for quick sex or instant cash, but for something more permanent and enduring. Caught in my own tailspin, I know I have not been the best father or husband this past year. But suddenly, more than anything, I need my family. My daughter's warm face cupped in my hands, my son's long limbs draped across mine, my wife's soft body on the sofa beside me. My obsessive focus on my own depression has obscured the one true thing in my life.

I get up and pack quickly. My friends will not understand, but I do. It's not freedom I miss, or youth, or beauty. It's the connection to people I love, the electric feeling of conversation, the human touch. In this place, those things can be simulated but never duplicated, while even the real thing disappears behind a veil of diversion and noise. I know now where I have to go. I write my friends a note, then shut the door quietly behind me. Home, I breathe. Home.

LOVE CHILD

by Anne Burt

Two weeks back from my honeymoon, I packed up my house and my daughter and my dog and moved into my new husband's house with his daughter and his dog. My clothes were in boxes, books in the basement, toys in the garage. The paint was still wet on the walls of our new attic bedroom. The ink was still wet on my divorce papers and on our marriage certificate. And the stick was pink.

Oh, no. No no no no no. I stared at the stick in utter disbelief: How could it betray me this way? The stick and I had had a codependent relationship for more than twenty years. I bought one whenever I was late, or feeling out of sorts, or questioning the direction my life had taken, or feeling the need to wonder: What if something completely spontaneous was to happen? I always held on to the stick for a few days before using it, because part of the experience was the anticipation of finding out the answer. Did something enormous, something ground-moving, sweeping, romantic, insane, just happen of its own accord?

A week into my second marriage, it seemed that it had.

The notion of spontaneity was antithetical to life in my first marriage. I never, I mean *never*, forgot to take my pill before bed. Take my pill, wash my face, brush my teeth, pajamas on, lights off. My only pregnancy to date had been completely planned. For my first marriage, I chose safety. Along with that, I chose a life of worry about doing everything right. I was worried all the time, insomniac, growing ancient in my early thirties.

Meeting my second husband changed all of that. We made plans—big, crazy plans. We made each other pursue our greatest dreams. I quit another so-so job in a long string of so-so jobs and got my first book contract. He patented his first two inventions. We were happy together—physically, intellectually, emotionally—and together, we made each other braver than either of us had been alone. The future sparkled. Forty never looked so good.

My second husband met me and his first sailboat within twenty-four hours of each other. He taught himself how to sail in the choppy waters of New York Harbor, scissoring his 1979 Hunter between the Staten Island Ferry and the freighters, bobbing in their wake between New York and New Jersey, watching the skyline light up at dusk. I hadn't sailed a day in my life before we met. For our honeymoon, inexperienced as we were, we decided to rent a sailboat for a week in the Caribbean. Why not? It was, like everything, a joyous adventure I never would have risked in my first, "safe," marriage. Instead, I felt safer than I ever had on the deck of a rented sailboat with my new husband, pitching up and down in the waves not ten feet from the sharp craggy rock formations of the caves of Virgin Gorda as we tried and failed and tried and failed to catch a mooring, nearly capsizing against the rocks on one side and front-ending a forty-foot Hobie Cat on the other. I trusted my husband, and trusted we would catch that mooring eventually.

When I had realized I would be getting my period while we honeymooned on the sailboat, I decided simply to flip the weeks on my pill packet, continuing the hormones on the period week and stopping them for the next. It seemed like the perfect solution. After all, these would be extra hormones, not fewer.

And now the stick was pink.

My husband's cabinet shop was less than five minutes away from our house. I climbed over boxes to find the phone and told him I had to come over right away. He was wearing one of the flannel shirts that had gone through the wash so many times that it had no texture left, just a layer of soft over him that smelled good, that always made me want to bury my face in his chest. Which is just what I did when he asked me, What's up?

I breathed in the shirt, then pulled back and looked at him.

"I'm pregnant," I said, and burst into tears.

Even as I cried, I was saying to myself: Oh, come on. You're a smart chick; you know how birth control works. Maybe you need to think about why you let yourself get pregnant. Maybe deep down you really do want to have another baby.

Still, I knew my motivations were not so black-and-white. Was flipping my pill packet incautious, even stupid? Yes. But was I trying to get pregnant? No. I just wanted to let myself stop worrying about making mistakes all the time. I wanted to fully embrace everything about the notion of "why not?" because the amazing miracle of my husband, our girls, my own happiness, seemed to come from my newfound ability to leap instead of look.

And yet, here was reality: We were almost forty, married less than a month, our daughters still acclimating to the monumental changes thrust upon them. I felt like I had fucked up royally, like I'd ruined the new life I wanted so much, and now I would have to pay for my lack of vigilance.

But I looked at my husband—and he was laughing at my shocking news. Laughing! I'd just turned his life upside down and he was laughing. And here again was the gift of this new marriage, of this man in my life: Mistakes weren't deadly. Life was fun. I couldn't destroy him; consequently, I hadn't destroyed myself. His arms were around me, his shirt was soft.

"I don't know if I want this baby," I whispered.

"I don't know if I do either," he said, "but look: Here's life. We're in it." Which, I realized after he said it, was exactly what I wanted him to say. I was afraid he'd be angry that I'd ruined our plans; when he wasn't, I felt flooded with hope, with love, with the sense that something marvelous had happened that was bigger than us and our plans. This was our chance, probably our last chance, to make a person together. I started to love this pregnancy not despite the fact that it was unplanned, but because it was unplanned, just like the miracle of the second half of my life. And sex with my new husband, which had been amazing from the start, became even better. Deeper, sexier. Like we had so much love that we had to make a whole new person to contain it all.

When we saw the obstetrician for our first sonogram, there it was. The beating heart. And God if it wasn't as exciting as the first time.

We made a heart, I said to my husband, already more than eager to get him home and do more of what got that heart there in the first place.

"I can't be sure with my equipment," my OB said, "but I wouldn't be surprised if this baby is a couple of weeks further along than you think." Which put conception at our honeymoon, on that sailboat rocking up and down in the waters off the British Virgin Islands when we had finally caught our mooring.

We told our daughters. At dinner, my husband showed the girls what our fetus looked like by holding up a piece of chicken and marking the heart with a black bean. His rendition was remarkably accurate. I could have been any mother cooing and obsessing over her miraculous ability to reproduce, but that's not the miracle that moved me to such heights this time around—it was the improbability of sitting around this table with my new family, unplanned, all of it, but giving me more love and happiness than I ever imagined. The dogs ran wild through the living room and the chaos they created was part of what I loved. I was carrying a love child.

"Your ass looks great in those jeans," my husband said as I bent down to load the dirty dishes in the dishwasher.

"See, that's what got us into this predicament in the first place," I answered. But I'd fully embraced the predicament, and felt no difference between the fun and its consequences. In my new marriage, everything was fun and all of it felt safe.

We had to take our little black-bean chicken to a radiology center where specialists had high-tech equipment for a super sonogram—with my "advanced maternal age," the OB wanted a more accurate reading of our due date. We joked about naming the baby "Island Girl," after the sailboat we'd rented, the place she was conceived. We wanted an *I* name, after my great-uncle Irving who had had us over in his kitchen for vodka tonics once a week before he died, who was the only relative other than my parents who had truly spent time with my husband and knew me in this new, happy marriage. I had already agreed to my husband's wish for a boy name: Isaac. Middle name

Newton. Why not? It made me laugh, in the right way, the happy way, the love child named for one of humanity's greatest outside-the-box thinkers. Not even the sky would limit this child. . . .

"I can't find the heartbeat," said the technician.

Her hand was over my belly, sliding the cold, gelled wand up and down, searching in the dark. The screen showed black and grey undulations, pulsing waves, caves. There was my chicken, but no black bean.

Sorry, she said as she snapped off the screen. She had appointments lined up out the door, stage-four cancer patients with weeks to live, frightened people with mysterious masses on their brains, in their bodies, to diagnose. She left the room.

That was it.

When the love child disappears, what happens to the love?

We grew up in our marriage a whole lot faster than we would have even with a new baby. We had both been through new parenthood before, but not this sobering loss. Was it inevitable that our buoyant, charmed second chance would come back to earth? Was the truth about life's disappointments such that our grand, incautious adventure was inevitably a temporary phase? I felt so alive in the love of my new marriage, yet we made death.

I had a D & C and I welcomed the anesthesia wholeheartedly: Yes, obliterate me, take me out of this even for an hour. Give me something to recover from, something physical and real. One month married and pregnant seemed insurmountable when the stick turned pink; four months married and miscarried made me wish it all back. Sure, it happened to women every day, especially at my age. But something else happened with it. We resumed our sex life after the necessary waiting period, but I no longer felt like a newlywed.

When I was pregnant the first time, in my first marriage, sex virtually stopped. This time, I had wanted sex always, through the morning sickness and various sorenesses and exhaustions. So sex after the love child died felt hollow and misfortunate for a while. I missed the love child too much. I switched to an IUD, preventing myself from playing loose and fast with conception. The IUD lasts five years; by that time, presumably, a baby won't really be an option for us without lots of technology and overdetermination—the opposite of incaution. And as time has passed, as our daughters reconciled themselves to their new family structure and started to bloom within it, as our sex life returned and bloomed again too, and as some of our grand plans have come to fruition and some, inevitably, haven't, I feel more and more certain that another baby is not in our future.

Our marriage is in its second year. If we were to have a child, now would be the time. But I realize that I don't, and never really did, long for a baby. What I longed for was the spontaneous life in which a love child was possible. That's what my incaution was about, and my husband—with his laughter and his strength and his glorious ability to say "Why not?" when all of our plans and dreams changed with a pink stick—has given me exactly what I wanted.

THE LEAST WE COULD DO

by Eric Bartels

Did sex bring my wife and me together? You decide.

I recall vividly the first time I saw her. I was working as a bartender, something I did for many years, the night she and her live-in boyfriend came into the place where I worked, taking a small table some distance from where I stood. She sat facing me, so that I was able to see the striking contrast between her ink black hair and perfect white skin, her cat eyes and her lush, full lips, which she had a habit of painting bright red in those days.

What followed remains the subject of a corny-sounding, oft-repeated debate, the kind the kids take a sort of squirmy delight in hearing. I tried to get a good look at her, in a respectful, exploratory way at first, because I've never been inclined to leer at women in the company of other men.

(I'd like to think I'm not inclined to leer at women at all, but I am prepared to say for the record that I do like the way women look.) I looked again, and, later, again, trying each time to read the angle of her face so I'd know when to avert my gaze, but at some point, we made eye contact. I'm sure I looked away quickly, because it's especially wrong to stare at a woman whose man has his back turned, but soon my eyes went back to her. Again she was looking at me.

This is the part of the story she dismisses as a fiction, but my memory is clear. Before long, she was the one looking with greater purpose. I had to shrink from her gaze. She had turned the tables. She had the hungrier eyes.

Some time after that night, she returned, this time to sit at my bar with the boyfriend and another male friend. Now we had met. The next time she came, it was alone. And then the boyfriend was gone. She was intelligent and witty and career-minded, self-possessed but with an agile, irreverent sense of her surroundings and the world. And up close, she was even more beautiful than I first thought. We'll call her Nancy, because that's her name.

But I'm leaving out the part about how I was living with someone at the time. It was a relationship that was trending downward, but I was unclear about what to do with it. I don't know if I was certain it would end at that point, but I had already ceased to be faithful to it or to her. Now I would step up the pace.

Nancy and I began seeing each other every week or two, almost exclusively at the restaurant, or at her place after

I'd finished work. Looking back, I suppose all of the processes that unfold in a conventional courtship were taking place: We learned each other's histories and aspirations. We evaluated each other's strengths and weaknesses. We met each other's friends. (I even met her youngest sister, who was about twelve at the time. She's thirty now.) We drank and laughed and talked. And we had sex. Not the loving, leisurely variety, but the kind that happens when powerful attraction and bad behavior come together. We had sex on bar stools. On tables. Standing up. Against walls. Any place big enough for two bodies and secret enough to hide us from the outside world. This went on for a year and a half, until the woman I lived with and I finally parted.

Soon now, Nancy and I will have known each other for twenty years and been married for ten. We have a daughter who's racing through elementary school and a son not far behind her. We own a modest home in a nice neighborhood, and, while we're not rich by any means, we've achieved a measure of comfort. I write feature stories for a newspaper and my wife works for a small advertising and public relations firm. In other words, we're a pretty conventional professional couple at or well into middle age. (She's at; I'm well into.)

Neither of us is exactly as physically fit as we'd like to be, but we're both active and healthy and benefit from good genes. I think it's safe to say that either would still attract attention if placed back on the open market, not that we have any such plans. And sometimes, when we have the time and the energy and the opportunity, we find each other and reclaim some of the hunger that brought us together nearly two decades ago. But it's taken some doing.

Over the course of our relationship, we've strained and struggled and often lost track of the mutual fascination we had at the beginning. Hell, forget about affection; we've had simple respect slip from our grasp. Some of it came as the predictable result of the at times harrowing process known as life, which in our case involves raising two kids and maintaining two careers. And some of it goes back farther.

Way back, when my ex-girlfriend and I split up, I was determined to play the field for a while. I'd been in a serious relationship for several years and was not looking for another. I told Nancy about this need for liberty, and she grudgingly played along. We continued to see each other regularly, and I realize now she was always my favorite, but I saw other women, and Nancy, of course, had similar freedom. She clearly had misgivings about the arrangement, but we remained a kind of item through three or four years of it. Then we moved in together.

Certainly, we thought of ourselves as a couple in the years that followed. We spent carefree time together, traveled and talked of marriage and children, although those discussions usually involved one or the other person pitching the idea only to be rejected in a mock serious way. But there were also real uncertainties about commitment, and the relationship was rocked on more than one occasion by infidelities. We survived, but in time our sex life lost some of its urgency. Complacency had crept in and I was the one, I saw later, who'd left the door open. I had allowed familiarity to disrupt my focus. I had come to take Nancy for granted.

When Nancy became pregnant with our daughter, it was no surprise. Discussions about a family had evolved into a rather informal understanding: If we got pregnant, we'd get married. When the time came, we were thrilled that we would be parents, but also glad, I think, to finally, formally be together. We invited a small number of family members and were married in a lush, quiet corner of a city park early one summer day as a climbing sun steamed away a morning mist.

I was now a new husband and soon-to-be father. What I didn't know was that our love life was about to undergo a transformation as well. The change would be simple. We would no longer have sex on my schedule, not that it was a terribly demanding regimen at the time. Now the physical and psychic demands pregnancy placed on Nancy meant I would be the one awaiting the call. I suppose it was the prospect of our first child and a newfound respect for the woman carrying it that gave me a willingness to embrace this new dynamic. That, and sheer ignorance of what lay in store. But I waited.

With access to Nancy limited, I figured I had better be fully ready when summoned. Toward that end, I made a rather bold lifestyle change, one whose impact I could not have imagined: I stopped masturbating. Now, don't get me wrong. I'm not saying our love life had been abysmal before and that it was due to some infantile compulsion on

my part. I don't think my habit had been any more pronounced than that of most guys, and I do mean guys in relationships. Like them, I would simply let off a little steam
from time to time. Facing a new reality, I thought I'd see
what happened if I kept myself fully charged all the time.

The difference was dramatic. Suddenly, our lovemaking
featured something that had been absent more often than I
had known: real ardor on my part. And I liked the feeling.
It wasn't so much that I was proud of my newfound devo-
tion, although there was an element of that. I had rediscov-
ered what it felt like to want my wife. Bad.

The obvious irony of this new desire, of course, was
that the very thing that created it also limited its practice.
Restricted access made me fonder, but then I had no place to
put my fondness. But I stuck to the program, preferring to
endure the discomfort of days and even weeks without sex
rather than allow myself to give Nancy less than my best on
the occasions when she had any use for it. The quality if not
the quantity of our lovemaking continued to improve. I now
felt an almost teenage eagerness for her and felt I was com-
bining it with the savvy of a veteran. Her sexual response
began to show new and exciting facets. Was I doing that?

But things would reach a turning point when Nancy
returned to work near the end of our daughter's first year.
I can't ever hope to fully understand the psychology or the
biology of womanhood, let alone motherhood. I can well
imagine that a woman's self-image is attacked and transformed by the latter. Before, she was a woman, which car-

ries its own set of complications. Now she was a mother, feeling a kind of attachment to and responsibility for her children that a father never completely shares. Then there's the whole matter of a career and the pressures that entails, and all this, in our case, for a woman who takes her responsibilities very seriously.

More than once, Nancy explained that my overtures at the end of a long day felt like just another demand on her time and energy. I tried to be empathetic, but I was working hard, too, and not just at my job. I had taken on a healthy share of the shopping, cooking, cleaning, and other responsibilities, and was a loving, attentive father. I realized that our life had put us on parallel tracks that increasingly never intersected.

Sex, for me, was beginning to represent a deeper connection that we were not making, yet it wasn't a priority for Nancy. It seemed that just as she was needing less, I was needing her more. And while I was feeling more and more mystified and hurt, her response to my entreaties, whatever approach I took, evolved from pained noncompliance to open disinterest to utter resentment and anger. She became so wary of potential advances on my part she began to recoil from my touch, and not just in the bedroom. Even innocent demonstrations of affection between us started to become rare.

On a visit with my sister's family, we learned that she and her husband, evidently battling the same issue, had spent months—and untold dollars—with a counselor. They were finally told to find a middle ground, a minimum number of times per week they would have sex. The number was one. This, they explained, took pressure off my brother-in-law, who would know that his dry spells would not be interminable. My sister, in turn, could relax without her husband constantly pestering her. Perfect, I told Nancy, they spent all the money asking the questions; we get the answer for free. She seemed to agree, but our difficulties persisted. A week would pass, and, trying to honor the idea that I not pressure my wife, I would hold my tongue. But additional days would go by and I would grow uneasy, sometimes physically. Didn't I read somewhere that bottling that stuff up will give you prostate cancer or something?

Now I began to chafe at my wife's seeming apathy toward the issue. Could so sexual a creature as the Nancy I had met years before have disappeared altogether? Did she care if we were still connected at all by intimacy? Did my needs mean nothing to her? I would've been content to have her fake an interest in sex. Not to be overly graphic, but there were times when anything would have worked: oral sex, a teenage-style hand job. I would ask my wife if she'd let me look at her body while I jerked off. Pretty desperate stuff.

I began averting my eyes when Nancy was undressing. The sight of her body was too much for me. There were times when I would sleep in the extra bedroom because I couldn't bear the thought of being next to her and yet unable to touch her. I figured I was more frustrated than the loneliest bachelor, because I couldn't use the excuse of not having a partner. My frustration grew. I began to return her lack of affection and would grow sullen, and when she ignored my silence, I'd get combative. Then we'd fight, and the ever so fragile chance for romance would shatter, completing a perfect cycle. And worst of all, our anger spilled out of the bedroom and into the rest of the house, where it could infect our young children with fear and uncertainty.

One of the great ironies in all this is that the once-a-week plan probably would have saved us years of acrimony. I've never thought of myself as a particularly prodigious sexual athlete. I have a healthy libido, but I've never been one to brag about going all night or doing it this or that many times in a row. I always felt that if you do it right the first time, everybody can go ahead and get some sleep. After a nice session of lovemaking, I barely think about sex for a couple days. Heck, do the math. Sex three times a week is probably at the outer edge of what I could handle. Twice would be good, but once a week—guaranteed—might indeed have kept the wolves at bay.

When our son was born, we learned the confounding arithmetic of the second child: the workload doesn't double, it expands exponentially. Our love life stayed on the back burner. I tried everything. I'd urge Nancy to look at sex as a wonderful treat, like a fun game or a rich dessert that we get to share at our whim. I don't think she got it. I encouraged her to return in her mind to the days when she associated sex with rebellion and adventure, as she almost certainly did when we first met. That didn't work either. Then I tried to panic her with talk of squandering the waning years of our physical beauty and full sexual abilities. Maybe she wasn't worried about it, but I had a right to be.

I'm approaching fifty, Nancy is forty-one, and while I can happily report that my readiness has not diminished yet, I don't know where I'll be, sexually speaking, in ten or fifteen or twenty years. And what if, at some point, it becomes a matter not of whether I can perform, but whether I'll be asked to? If she doesn't want me now, why would she want a more decrepit version later? Or suppose she drops me after the kids are grown and gone. How much demand is there for modest-net-worth, retirement-age guys?

A very slow-moving miracle began to unfold in our relationship. Battle fatigue and time came to our rescue. I've decided that couples cease fighting not because they reach an agreement on issues that divide them, but because they simply tire of fighting. And my wife and I fought over this one plenty. Yet the passage of time has been the real key. With the kids growing older and more self-sufficient, it seems Nancy's burden has lifted a bit. Although she'll now hold me off by saying, "It hasn't even been a week," adopting the guideline she wouldn't honor before, things are better. Looking back, I don't know if anything could've been done to improve the situation when it was at its worst. Maybe the only answer is to somehow make sure that anyone considering a family should do so only with the very clear understanding that they might well see their love lives on the back burner for a year or two. Or eight. But then, at the risk of sounding unkind, that's their problem now.

Our kids are perfectly comfortable staying home with the sitter these days, so my wife and I have started going out on a regular basis. We do fun things and have a drink or two, which takes us back to a place we once knew well, where cares are put aside for a time and the point is to be together. That place looks and feels a little different now, mostly because of what we bring to it. After nearly twenty years, there is a foundation beneath us, one built from the satisfaction of standing at someone's side as time sweeps by, carrying giddy elation and searing pain and everything in between.

Whether we're always aware of it or not, we make love on that foundation now, and here's the best part: It's not Hallmark-card love. I hate that silly myth about the quiet, steady kind of companionship that invariably replaces mystery and excitement in a relationship of many years. Other couples can make that choice if they like. No, we're still sneaking around, although now it's so the kids won't catch us. And we make love a lot like we did at the very beginning: hungrily and messily and sometimes a bit impolitely. That makes me happy for obvious reasons, but it also makes another fantasy possible. In this one, our children are grown, and as we watch them reach for whatever dreams they've imagined for themselves, we realize that we've weathered storms bravely enough to give them that chance. At that point, maybe we'll look at each other, wordlessly but with the same thought in mind: Not bad for two people who were just in it for the sex.

LOVE AND BAD LANGUAGE
by Marion Winik

One hundred and forty days ago, I met you in a bookstore in Maryland. Not that night, but the next time we were in the same state—exactly ten days later— we slept together, and we have again every time we could after that. Twenty-four times.

This is only 17 percent of the time, and our average is getting worse. The last time I saw you was seven days ago, and I will not see you again for thirty more. It will be our longest separation so far, longer than our previous record by a whole week.

Most nights we sleep more than 1,650 miles apart.

So it began, and how it went on!—this inflamed and

shameless essay, written for the online literary-smut magazine Nerve.com. It embarrasses me a little to read it now, with its show-off talk of parts and juices and golden hair. Doubtless you can still find it on the Internet; my grandchildren's grandchildren will probably be able to read it, unless the Republicans finally get their hooks into cyberspace.

As I threw myself into a fourteen-month long-distance romance with the man I met in the bookstore in Maryland, Crispin Sartwell, Ph.D., philosopher, anarchist, blues harmonica player, newshound, improbable atheist Jew, he came with me, even gave me a run for my money, in e-mails, in op-ed columns, in lectures addressed to undergraduate classes, in a partner essay for Nerve.com, in an encomium delivered at my going-away party when I left Texas and also at our wedding in Pennsylvania. The cataclysm of our courtship is as well documented as only a romance between two writers can be, and if there are two writers more prone to literary exhibitionism than we, they probably are not married.

As I write these lines, it is 2,643 nights since we met, and our "percentage," as I referred to it then, has gotten much, much better: We celebrated the sixth anniversary of what is a second marriage for both of us in June. But what has become of OGL—Our Great Love, once so frequently discussed it required an acronym—in that time has happened largely in silence.

In silence on the page, anyway. Our house has been torn by vicious arguments, scornful comments, wild shouts, and raging diatribes, cases prosecuted with extreme prejudice by two people using the same unrestricted access to the English language as they did when they were proclaiming their love to the world. It has taken its toll. This week I wondered to a friend of mine if there is any difference in the actual degree of conflict or type of problems suffered by the divorced and the not divorced. Maybe it's just that some people will stay together almost no matter what, I said wearily, and maybe Crispin and I are just that kind of people. (While he has managed to get divorced once, I am widowed: I've escaped, so far, only by death.)

In describing the origin of this bitter debate, I will be brief: The last thing I am trying to do is continue the argument here. While Crispin and I have the usual couple problems—one careful with money, one not so much; one constitutionally opposed to clutter, one rather fond of it; at odds over bed linens and grocery-shopping procedures and toilet paper rolls—we have the interpersonal skills to live with these differences, to negotiate compromises, to tolerate their abandonment, to try a little harder next time. To laugh about it. *My goodness, Marion*, says the caption of the curling, yellowed *New Yorker* cartoon posted above our sink. *These dishes are so spotless I can see deep within my hollowed, tortured soul.*

The issue that has torn us apart is sexual jealousy, and, at least from my point of view, it has no basis except in the past. His past (searing betrayals and violations lodged deep in the soft tissue) and my past ("finding myself" in the seventies and eighties, then writing four books about it). Crispin would agree, I think, that no transgression of monogamy has occurred in our history together, yet this matter has been driving us crazy for seven years—if I go out of town alone, if I talk to an old boyfriend, if I wear a low-cut shirt, if some ancient foolishness comes up in a discussion with old friends. I have managed to contradict myself many times in my frantic attempts to defend myself, causing him to dismiss not only my potential for loyalty but also my integrity. Neither Al Gore nor John Kerry merited as much scorn as I (and I defended them as if they were me). God save us from elections.

Some days I am incandescent with ardor, with Our Great Love: OGL, as we call it in our e-mail shorthand, where xs are kisses, os are hugs, and ys are blow jobs. Some days I am lit from within, hot and bright and transparent as a kerosene lamp. Like a nun, burning with unconsummated passion, with holy fire.

Other days, I feel like a person whose body is rejecting an organ transplant. There are times when the lost, hungry feeling of not being with you sucks up every bit of space in my lungs and brain. Your absence is bigger than any presence.

We have always been very good spellers, Crispin and I; we are book lovers, we are graphomanes, and our crime of choice is the verbal equivalent of domestic violence, like the characters in the famous Edward Albee play. Be afraid of Virginia Woolf, be very afraid, for no matter how you wish it, no cruel word can be unsaid.

The experience of living in the closest possible proximity to someone you feel bitterly alienated from is not an uncommon one for married people. Even people who don't begin by describing their sexual combustibility on the Internet and follow that up with getting each other's initials tattooed on their bodies have to deal with coming down from the euphoria of early romance, finding themselves cranky and critical and not getting just what they need. A fair number of them probably face issues that come straight from the heart of the love, like ours do, issues of trust and acceptance and interdependence.

And yet, and yet, and yet. And yet what survives of Our Great Love 2,643 days out is a surprising amount, I think, particularly in the bedroom. Those blue eyes I rhapsodized about with help from Roget in my Nerve.com essay—they still have the power to transfix me, often suddenly, while I'm smoothing a sheet or ladling soup. Though some of the ferocious passion that fueled OGL seems to have been diverted to other pursuits, or has perhaps caved in on itself—I mean the ferocious passion of the fighting, the tiny, megalomaniac departments of defense—our stripped-down and efficient lovemaking still works so well I doubt either one of us would ever give it up. In addition to knitting us back together on a quotidian basis, sex has produced even more effective glue: a now-five-year-old daughter.

It brought us together, it drives us apart, and it contributes to the rescue effort again and again, which kind of wears you out after a while. Perhaps the two-faced quality of our physical connection adds to biological reasons for the fact that we (now closing in on fifty) are a bit less obsessed with it in than we were in the Nerve.com period. There are pleasures that mean as much to us now as the loin-generated ones. On our good days, we laugh at each other's jokes, enjoy each other's conversation, respect each other's minds, cherish an image of growing old that includes the other. Because I work at home and Crispin is a college professor, we spend much more time together than most couples our age, and most of these hours are spent in quiet harmony—or not-so-quiet harmony, as, in addition to the five-year-old, we each brought two kids into the marriage who are teenagers now.

When I look around this house, this town, this life, everything feels surreal. My surroundings are exactly as they were before I knew you, yet my interior landscape is rearranged as if by an earthquake. A few new photographs on the refrigerator don't tell the story. And the daily round of work, kids, meals, carpools, soccer games feels like a charade.

Why are we cooking two different dinners in two different houses in two different states? Something is wrong with this picture, don't you see? About three months ago, I said to you: My home is where you are. Well, now I say it again. My home is exactly only where you are.

You want begging, I'll give you begging.

Because the sound of you breathing when you come on the phone is good, but it is not enough.

At times now I fear we experience allegiance to the idea of our love more than we experience the love itself. But a love like this deserves allegiance, I believe.

Recently I read a line in Bee Lavender's memoir *Lessons in Taxidermy:* "If this was love, it seemed to be about reciprocity and disciplined attention to details." This was written from the point of view of a young woman so marked by illness and tragedy that she never had the out-of-the-heart-springing-crazy sensation I know as falling in love; she determines that she is in love almost as an alien would in a sci-fi movie, by evaluating the details of her situation among the earthlings, the fact that she is treating someone with caring and carefulness and he is responding in kind, and then saying, Hey, this must be it.

There's a lesson for Crispin and Marion in that, I think. But here on day 2,643, I look at the way our bodies still work together, and our minds, and our lives, and I say the same thing: Hey, this must be it.

SOPHOCLES, BUDDHA, MARION, AND ME

by Crispin Sartwell

⌒⌒⌒ *The first of the Buddha's fourfold truths is that life is suffering. The second is that suffering is caused by desire. Desire hurts by definition because it means you don't have what you want. Even so, people want desire itself. If people didn't want to want, they wouldn't spend all that money on aphrodisiacs. Men don't want orgasms; we want erections.*

So I'm recommending an inverted Buddhism: finding nirvana through desire, heightening it, deepening it, gloating over it, immersing ourselves in it by deferring its gratification.

Our deferral makes us make words, and our words have been fucking since we met. Our phone calls are sex: voices wandering in the low octave of want. Our e-mail is sex. Our letters are sex. Our magazine pieces are sex. We wouldn't need these words, couldn't find them, without the intensity that being apart gives to our wanting.

When I was twenty or so I had a friend named Michael who managed to sleep with every pretty girl on the Eastern Seaboard. The threesomes with the gorgeous bisexual models and so on were astounding in their scope and frequency. Then Michael fell in love with a girl who I think could generously be described as dumpy, and they got married and moved to Omaha. I asked him, approaching the topic delicately, how he could get from there to here. And he said: "It doesn't matter how they look. When you're in bed with a body, it's *the* body; this is the woman now and forever. I'm going to be exactly as into it, because, every time, I'm going to be completely into it."

I've been thinking about that for a quarter century, and certainly in the seven years since I wrote my essay for Nerve.com in the first raptures of lust for Marion Winik. It is an unusual attitude in a man raised in our culture, where images of the bodies of girls bombard both men and women in every waking hour. My desires were fed on pornography and cover girls, on lingerie catalogs and television stars, and every woman was understood visually and desired in proportion to the standards thus embodied. Among other things, how the woman you're with looks is an element of your prestige; it's a way heterosexual men establish a little, as it were, pecking order. The way a woman looks takes her outside herself or places her beside herself; it becomes an element of male egomania, a way to manufacture status.

What Michael had figured out was how to love real women, from models to the sweet-but-chubby. And I think that maybe that's why even the models wanted to sleep with him—he wasn't sleeping with them because they were models. I lost track of Michael in deepest Omaha, but it wouldn't shock me to find out that the marriage is going pretty well.

What Michael knew in 1980, I have learned—slowly, intermittently, with difficulty—since. As I have proceeded through the stages of life's way, my tastes in women have kept pace. When I was a teenager I kissed teenagers. When I was in grad school studying philosophy, nothing seemed sexier to me than scholars in their first intellectual bloom. A neurotic twenty-five-year-old struggling to interpret Hegel's *Phenomenology of Spirit* is, after all, a creature of unadulterated torturous loveliness.

When I was raising small children, my eyes would stray to young mothers at the playground. They seemed so focused on their little ones and yet so . . . distractible. And I'm now a bit of a connoisseur of crow's-feet and gravelly voices; every woman worth her salt is, by the time she reaches my present age (pushing fifty), a sexual veteran, and perhaps she's lost a little bit of the confusion, not to say desperation, that sometimes characterizes the young American woman with regard to matters sexual. Women at fifty are often pretty sure who they are, which can be extraordinarily irritating, or not. The fact that I have to say this should not distract you from its truth: I find my wife, the lovely yet challenging Marion, as sexy as I did the day I first . . . met her. Sexier.

Probably we've both lost some of our urgency. Certainly our skin has lost some elasticity. And though I've had some trouble making peace with my aging body—its embarrassing paunch and recalcitrance to athletic will—I've had no trouble making peace with Marion's: I like the way she inhabits it or has achieved identity with it, and, to boot, her breasts are still lovely.

I do not credit myself for this perspective, because it is hardly a matter of decision; the pointer acts on its own, a divining rod. But it is a very good thing, because when a man's taste in bodies does not mutate as his own body does, he becomes some sort of sex offender. I'm sending a daughter off to college; she has friends. My eighteen-year-old son has a pretty girlfriend, whom we refer to around here as Soccer Barbie. And this semester I am, like most others, teaching about fifty female undergraduates. It is not that I am immune to perfect nubility, but my appreciation has gained a certain aesthetic distance; I'm not tortured or even, usually, particularly impressed. As your body ages, your senses have to age too: your seeing has to age, or seeing is a sickness.

I think it's fair to say that the seeing sickness is very, very common among American hetero men, our very own STD.

But I should say, taking it from the other angle, that being seen can also be a sickness.

It is hard for me not to notice that the Western woman, overall, is, in her deepest personal identity, an exhibitionist. Without this exhibitionism, the economy, among other things, would collapse, and sexual relations would have to be entirely reconstrued. But the mode of appearance must be allowed to mature along with the body being displayed, or else a woman ends up, not as a sex criminal, but as a deeply embarrassing spectacle, the female version of the dirty old man. Gail Sheehy recently published a book dedicated to the sexiness of women around sixty, and she posed for publicity photos in a tight leather outfit, looking at herself in a mirror like the *Rokeby Venus*. That's not about the sexiness of sixty-year-old women; it's about the pitifulness of pretense. It's despair, loss that cannot be accepted, desperation.

Of course, men have got a problem along these lines as well. In the beginning of the *Republic*, Plato quotes the great playwright Sophocles, in old age. "How do you feel about love," Sophocles is asked, "are you still capable of it?" "Hush! if you please: to my great delight I have escaped from it, and feel as if I had escaped from a frantic and savage master." And this is certainly an aspect of my own aging: I think as a younger man I experienced every aspect of my life in relation to sexual desire, and though I still have desire, it doesn't usually have me. I haven't reached the Sophocles stage, but halfway there is, overall, a relief. However, men now regard it as their right to be just as hard just as often as they were at sixteen, and probably Cialis is a very good complement to the sexagenarian Venus.

None of us, male or female, seem to want to let our sexuality change, but it changes anyway without us and leaves us incomprehensible to one another. If your choice is between a real and a simulated twenty-five-year-old, the only rational choice is trophy wife/boy toy.

The Japanese have a phrase that encompasses both a mature beauty and a mature seeing: *wabi-sabi,* or, struggling toward a direct translation, poverty and loneliness. It's the beauty of things that are old and disintegrating, things that are cracked and asymmetrical, things that are modest and typical. As opposed to the spring bud, *wabi-sabi* is the beauty of the late-autumn leaf after yellow and orange have given way to brown, just before the first wicked wind of the winter.

Buddhism encourages you to quiet your desires, holds that to be the only path to happiness. And though I personally would not want to be without desire, quieting is good, overall. For one thing, desire that is not a screaming need leaves you free to focus, leaves it possible for you to understand and know and actually appreciate its object. Perhaps if you did not desire at all, you would not see anything: The Buddhists call that nirvana. But a seeing that is driven by overwhelming desire is also a form of blindness. What I want is a real and modest seeing, a seeing under which desire can be transformed into love, into a cherishing of my wife and my world.

For one thing, the way I see Marion now is closer to whole. This involves an awareness of "faults," from imperiousness and excessive frugality to wrinkles and graying hair. Coming to know someone day by day for a decade can leave you with few illusions, and on some days with little charity or patience. But our lovemaking, for me, is a declaration that the faults themselves are inextricable from the beauty and truth of a whole person, an affirmation of asymmetry and disintegration, a love for what passes and a continual embracing of the process of living that we are engaged in together. And it's a good way to put off taking out the trash.

This idea of acceptance and self-acceptance is one way into the idea of maturity. But you've got to understand the paradox of acceptance: that accepting yourself changes your relation to yourself, for example. In this sense, self-acceptance is the precise opposite of self-esteem, the product that is most universally marketed to women, and that is now increasingly marketed to men, in the form of the hard-on tablet, among other things. Self-esteem is the incredible simulation of teenage tits dangling on your chest or your nonstop rock-hard erection. Self-acceptance is living with your cracked surface and your middle-aged paunch (damn it), your half-hard dick.

What bothers me about women, and one of the things that bothered me about Marion when I first met her, is a kind of lack of steadiness or stillness, a lack of balance, a lack of intrinsicness or inherence. But I might observe at the absurd level of absolute stereotype that women, especially young women, seek their reality outside themselves, as if it's all pushed to the surface of the body, to the skin, and then actually dematerialized into the air around them. At that point they lack, among other things, a point of view. Regaining this, or recovering it, pulling it back inside and stilling it just a little, becoming something actual and individual: These are the things that aging offers women. And to me, saying that that process is sexual or that that state of being is sexy states the obvious.

That is what I want: you, baby, not your wanting me to complete you or make you over into something worthwhile, but your completeness as it finally begins to form, as you retract into yourself and begin to smile, not at me or them but from within yourself; the truth you are, not the impression you dedicate your life to conveying. It's kind of cool, at least for a while, to be needed, but what is better than that is to be loved, for your partner to exist, and for the reaching to start from within herself, not back into herself from your eyes. There she ceases to be fundamentally a spectacle. To be honest, that would make monogamy, as I understand it, possible, both ways around.

I am a jealous man, and my jealousy focuses not primarily on whether my partner is sleeping with someone else (though that would be ample grounds for the end) but in the way my partner makes herself visible to other men, or wants to make herself visible to other men, or wants to create a sexual spectacle, or wants to take off her shirt and dance on a table. Let's just say that I've oppressed every woman with whom I've been in a serious relationship along these lines, Marion most of all. But women's desire to expose themselves like that is somewhat reduced by the time they get to fifty, and to me that makes it increasingly possible to love.

It is, of course, like all these things, a complementary system of mirrored dysfunctions. Perhaps my problem is precisely an excess of inherence; my oppression of women arises because my point of view is always merely from within myself, a lack of genuine connection or empathy. This problem is partly due to a selfhood that believes itself to be under attack or siege by women, a self that's always being colonized so that it reflects back at women the way they want to be seen or appreciated. But if you withdraw just that little bit from my head, perhaps I can follow, and instead of infesting each other we can share a bed together or actually enter into each other's bodies freely: the authentic French kiss.

Sex for me at this point is getting . . . simplified, and if I had to characterize my sex with Marion, I'd start with that. It is incredibly simple and direct: sex with my wife and in my life has lost its fraughtness. The insane self-consciousness by which we each try to monitor the other's attitudes or pleasures minute by minute, or the various ideas of what we could be or should be doing, the temptation of elaborate kinks, the exploration of a thousand fetishes: All this has kind of fallen away, leaving a crystalline center of pure fucking.

I've never been particularly interested in sleeping around,

or perhaps I've been interested but I haven't been able to actually try. Despite a few fairly extended single periods, I've slept with exactly eight women, and exactly one in the past ten years; they were all at least serious candidates for enduring love. This tends to make my opinions on these matters a bit suspect; other guys know a lot more about sex than I do, in a certain sense. But merely calming down a bit has cured me, by and large, of this pathetic exercise of comparing conquests or of wishing I had slept with all the women Michael slept with while at the same time disliking the whole idea. It's not that I wouldn't crack the swimsuit issue, but I probably wouldn't buy it, and it wouldn't engorge me without manual transmission. What I like most about my sex life now is that my fantasies and my realities have converged and merged, along with our bodies. Marion's body is the body, and I love even and particularly the signs of its aging, which are of course the signs of my own aging too. And I love the truth and decency of our sex, which is not to say it doesn't get pretty damn hot some afternoons. I have made love with Marion hundreds and hundreds of times; I intend to make love to her hundreds and hundreds of times more.

The sex in my head is a lot simpler than it once was, a lot more direct. I'd be lying if I said that I have no ambivalence about that, but I'd be lying if I said it wasn't a relief and a release from a frantic and savage master. It gives access to different dimensions of beauty—in women and in everything else. I learn to love the world by learning to love my woman.

Part II

SEXUAL EVOLUTION

THE JOY OF NOT
GIVING A DAMN

by Susan Cheever

When I was twenty-three, I married an older man. In bed and out of bed we were good friends, and the novelty of regular, legal, socially sanctioned sex surprised and delighted me every day and every night. It felt very grown up to be living in Greenwich Village with a thirty-one-year-old Harvard man who wore Brooks Brothers blue oxford cloth boxers under the suit he put on for work in a Midtown office, a man who knew his way around the confusing diagonal streets off Washington Square and the antipasti and linguine on the menu of the local Italian restaurant.

We lived in a Waverly Place apartment that my husband had sublet from a famous artist, and I felt that I was playing the role of the young married New Yorker, and playing it well. One spring night we met a couple, college friends of my husband's, for dinner at the Riviera Bar. As we chatted over hamburgers with chunks of iceberg lettuce and cold pitchers of draft beer, I examined the woman's face in the dim light of the restaurant. I could mercilessly pick out the inevitable, sad signs of her aging—the slight etched lines around her mouth, the faded skin of her cheeks, the web of crow's-feet when she laughed. She and her husband bickered over their summer plans, and I thought, No wonder! At her age she had probably stopped having sex. She was twenty-seven.

As an adolescent I longed for sex even before I understood exactly what it was. It had been explained to me in whispers by my schoolmates and in halting medical language by my parents. I was a very hungry teenager: hungry for sex, for power, for love, for recognition, and for food, to name just a few of the many things I desperately wanted.

My sex life before I was married, while I was in my late teens and early twenties, had been a scary series of illicit incidents. Abortion was terrifying in those days before the 1973 *Roe v. Wade* decision made it legal, and birth control was hard to get. A high school classmate of mine had mentioned in passing one day that she thought she might be pregnant; after that day she disappeared from school and I never saw her again. No one even mentioned her name. I was afraid to ask.

When my first boyfriend and I approached what I

imagined would be real sexual intercourse, I panicked. I could see that we were in the grip of overwhelming urges, but I knew what happened to girls who got pregnant. I visited a second-floor office of Planned Parenthood on the West Side of Manhattan during my lunch hour. I was working at a summer job at *Time* magazine, and my friends there had advised me to wear a fake engagement ring from Woolworth's. I wore the ring, but something about me tipped them off. I sat there under the eyes of the Planned Parenthood ladies, sweating bullets and pretending to search through my bag for a wedding invitation that wasn't there.

They refused to prescribe birth control. I squirmed in my wooden chair under their disapproving glare and tried to hide the waves of shame and humiliation that seemed to be billowing over me from the casement windows of the little office. Later that summer I acquired a bootleg diaphragm, but each sexual experience, even with a longtime boyfriend, combined a dose of danger, embarrassment, and intense fear with the physical pleasures of sex.

With the twin fears of pregnancy and loss of reputation howling around us, it's a miracle that anyone my age ever had any sex at all. The fear of pregnancy was powerful, but the fear of being a slut, of being "hard" or "used" or "loose" or "the kind of girl who went all the way," was almost worse. Stories about what happened to girls who let boys sleep with them were imaginative and horrifying. The boys in these stories were always animals; the girls were idiots. Our job as girls was to get men to want to marry us, and sex was our primary tool. We were warned again and again not to waste our sexual power without getting what we wanted. Enjoyment of sex might impair our ability to use it as leverage.

I insisted that my first boyfriend in college ask me to marry him before we slept together. He was reluctant, but I made his life miserable until he agreed. Marriage to this particular boyfriend seemed hugely impractical, but at least I could consider myself engaged. Under these circumstances, marriage as soon as possible seemed like a brilliant idea and a necessary step to adult freedom. As a result, once I managed to actually get married, regular, missionary-position sex seemed so exciting that it never occurred to me that there was anything else in the world. Although my husband had had some sexual experience before he met me, this kind of sex seemed to be all that occurred to him as well. No wonder. Compared to what I had grown up with—the clandestine, guilty gropings, the fear and inhibition—what we had was pure pleasure. I had achieved the main thing I needed to achieve in my lifetime as a woman—I was married. I had a wedding ring from Tiffany and stationery with my married name embossed at the top. I could relax at last.

I now see that I didn't know the first thing about pleasure. I'm not even sure if I was enjoying the sex as much as I was enjoying the freedom and acceptance that came with being married. My experience has been that as I have grown older, my physical relationships with men have grown emotionally less important and physically more pleasurable. As my hunger has waned with age and accomplishment, my sex life has become luminously full.

Looking back at my immensely pleasurable encounters with men over the years, I can see a few major shifts. The shift from guilt and fear to the ease and convenience of marriage was only the first. Then there was a shift from wanting men for who they were to wanting men for what they were. Even while I was married and in my thirties, I saw an agenda behind every man. I was a woman, and men were my ticket to ride. I fell in love with men over and over, and not just with their smells and funny ways of smiling or their wit and intelligence. I also fell in love with their achievements and their connections, and their great big wonderful lives. I wanted everything they had to offer me, and sometimes the fantasy of what that might be like was more powerful than my attachment to an individual man. After I became a journalist—something that happened largely because of my first husband's generosity in teaching me to write and edit—I fell in love with three of the most exciting journalists I knew.

It seemed like a privilege to watch as W. interviewed a former CIA operative, first getting him suitably drunk and then pretending that he knew more than he did in order to elicit new information. It was Watergate days, and these were the new techniques. It seemed an amazing thing to eavesdrop as C. did his methodical interviews, interviews in which he never took notes but later found a quiet place to write down everything he remembered, interviews that were the basis of his magnificent *New Yorker* profiles.

I was still hungry in those days, and my hunger for knowledge, for professional success, and for understanding was completely intertwined with my hunger for sex. A man's body and all the hot and cold, sinking and soaring feelings that it provided was also the physical manifestation of his mind, his accomplishments, and his status. I learned to write by marrying three writers. In a world before MFA programs, that seemed like the easiest way. Through my husbands and my lovers whole new worlds opened to me. I toured the World War I battlefields of northern France and read the astonishing works of Wilfred Owen and Robert Graves a few miles from where they were written. I met contemporary artists and began to understand their work. I got an intoxicating dose of politics when my husband ran for mayor of the city where we lived. Sex took me inside these worlds, granted me the access I never would have had on my own. Sex put me in the catbird seat. The gifts brought to me by these men were so huge that my prudery fell away. I discovered pleasures that I had thought were exclusively for prostitutes, things I had only read about or—after we all went to see *Deep Throat*—seen in the movies.

Through my third husband I met Jim and Artie Mitchell, two brothers who were famous for making the classic film *Behind the Green Door* and who ran a pornography theater in San Francisco. When Jim Mitchell shot and killed his brother I covered the trial and tried to write a book about their rise and fall. We hung out at the theater, a major San Francisco stop for savvy journalists, and I often got to enjoy the shock value of giving out-of-towners the inside tour through the locker rooms.

One of the great strokes of luck in my life—and there have been many—was to live through the golden years of the early 1970s when many of us women believed that sex should be free, that sex was the best way to get to know someone, and that sex was delicious physically but meaningless emotionally. Many women I knew decided that the differences between women and men were socially conditioned and abandoned those differences at the bedroom door. In my twenties and thirties I had somehow felt—even after all that time—that sex was something I was giving away. I still thought I had something to protect. As my body aged and I imagined that the value of what I was giving away began to plummet, the value of the mutual pleasure I might share began to accrue.

Then, just when I might have been winding up my sexual experience—as I turned fifty and separated from my third husband, leaving myself with two children to raise—I discovered a new level of sexual pleasure and a new kind of freedom. For the first time, I was not interested in the man's success or financial assets or what he could teach me; for the first time, I felt that I had nothing to protect. Instead, I felt that we were sharing an adventure. I wanted to try everything, and the lover I found was a more than adequate teacher. Fueled by the days and hours I spent raising my kids and supporting them, my attachment to my lover's apartment became a connection to a private fantasy world where nothing was off-limits. There was less love—we didn't really have much in common—and more sex than I had ever experienced. There was nothing I wanted from him except his companionship in bed.

I remember lying there one afternoon after making love and feeling as if the air was thick with the freedom I had found at last. The late-afternoon sun slanted through the windows onto the bookcases. I had to get up soon and take a shower and pick up my kids. Still, I reveled in the purity of the moment's physical delight. I didn't want to get married. I didn't need help in my career; I didn't need anyone else's money. I didn't want to have children. I wasn't quietly angling for this man's apartment, his connections, or his fortune. There was a purity to the bond I had with the man dozing next to me that I had finally earned. A year later, when the relationship ended in a blaze of bad behavior and tears and pain, as relationships sometimes do, I didn't really miss anything but the sex.

These days, my sexual relations with men are calmer and less at the center of my life. The actor Dustin Hoffman said that when he turned sixty-five, he began to feel that he was no longer "chained to a maniac." "There's a climate change inside you," he added. I'm not sixty-five yet, but after three marriages and many lovers, I know all the different things that sex can be and I have a kind of sexual freedom that I couldn't even have dreamed about back in my twenties. I believe that sex is a wonderful gift, a divine pleasure, a gorgeous way of connecting with another human being. It's not the prelude to marriage or a way to learn how to write or a way to get the rent paid.

My children have grown up in a world of legal abortion and sexual openness. These freedoms are under attack, but we are still a long way from the punishing assumptions of the 1950s and early 1960s. As I finish this essay late at night, I walk down the hall to the kitchen for a snack. I am still a hungry woman sometimes. As I pass my sixteen-year-old son's bedroom I look in on him, a man asleep with his arms thrown wide above him and his faithful dachshund curled next to one bent knee. What will physical relationships with men and women be like in this next generation? I hope that they will have the freedom of old age while they are still young enough to enjoy it.

MAN VERSUS MACHINE
by Kate Meyers

I used to be pretty adept at self-service. Never even considered using anything artificial. The men in my life were always more than willing to oblige, and when they weren't around I had no trouble taking care of my own business. The closest I came to an actual material encounter was when I moved in to the Hell's Kitchen apartment of my now ex-husband and found a vibrator in a paper bag under the sink. It was a sad imitation of a *Star Wars* phaser or laser or whatever they call it, in white plastic. It was also the last remnant of his previous relationship. Besides wanting any reminders of past inhabitants away, away, away, I was kind of skeeved by the thing. I deposited it in the garbage can without so much as a discussion. That was eleven years ago.

Two children and a divorce later, things have changed. On a recent girls' getaway, a friend asked me if I had a "home helper." I had never heard the term before, but, well . . . who couldn't use a little help at home? Shortly after, another girlfriend—married, I might add—and I were having a sex discussion, or lack-of-sex discussion, and I asked her about home help. "It's changed my life," she said with unabashed enthusiasm. I wasn't surprised by this information, just a bit shocked that she had kept it quiet. "I didn't know what to get but I surfed the Internet and bought three," she said. "I'm going to send you the one I like best." There is something so beautiful about friendship above and beyond the call of duty.

I know I was still a bit uncomfortable about the introduction of a sex toy into my life. But I liked the idea of it. It felt liberating and funny at the same time. And I loved shocking people with the information that I had crossed over into the realm of the battery-operated. Sometimes, my volunteering the information brought back information in return. One girlfriend, also recently divorced, discussed a gals' weekend in Las Vegas that she had recently participated in and that included a serious toy-shopping binge. As she was passing through airport security on her way home one of the gentlemen in charge of bag inspection asked, "Do you have a bob?" To which my friend replied, "A what?" and he explained, "A battery-operated boy." She was, of course, mortified. But it provided us with great laughs over cabernet and a wonderful new term in our artificial-helper lexicon. This all happened before I was a card-carrying bob owner myself.

My boy finally showed up. He arrived via UPS in a basic brown box, and inside the box was another box with a kind of see-through window. Printed on the top was a name, DOC JOHNSON. I opened it and pulled out a flesh-colored silicon object that looked remarkably like a penis—lifelike ridges and all. Underneath the window on the box were the words in bold print THIN COCK. Let me pause right here, right now, to say that I hope I never, ever, ever have to experience what these folks would dub a medium.

Anyway, once I got beyond the sizing shock, I had a flash: Doc Johnson will hold his stiffness forever, which sure beats any guy—even one who's having a bad reaction to Viagra. I can't call him Doc, though, because that was my dad's name, and the Freudian implications would cost me several college educations' worth of therapy, so I call him by his full name, Doc Johnson.

At first, I was afraid to take him out of the box. It was like when I moved to New York and it took me a few days to get up my courage to brave the subway. But I got over it. So . . . Doc Johnson takes two double-A batteries, and you're supposed to clean him after use. Right there, he's cheaper than a guy and less mess. No stickiness on the sheets or aftermath drips in the undies. Doc is one no-muss, no-fuss helper.

I don't remember when I first pulled him out to experiment, but I do remember the sensation. It was like "Good night, Irene" and "Uh, huh" and the best Lucinda Williams moan you could imagine. Wow, I thought, this guy is giving and giving, and I don't have to give back. It's all about me, and I don't have to talk or give directions or approvals or worry that I'm not doing enough of either. I am in total control. I don't wonder if it was good for Doc Johnson, and, better yet, it's *always* good for me. What guy has a track record like that? On top of it, Doc is so efficient. Knows exactly where to go, and how long to stay there. Just turn him on and voilà, one more thing to cross off my to-do list. No messing with foreplay or having to discuss my day. Doc Johnson is all action and no talk. I have never met a man like that.

So what can't Doc Johnson give me? Well, let's compare him to the first man I slept with after I left my husband. I met him—the man—on a business trip. A golf tournament, if you must know. And though I'm not flattered by the attention of men on golf outings (the ratio is like six zillion men to every skirt in spikes), this guy was severely charming, funny, intelligent, and black. Already, four things that my home helper was not. He gave good repartee, which is always fun, and when I like a man it's all about what's above the neck, not below the belt—so he had a huge advantage here. He also stank at golf, which I found extremely refreshing because, though I write about the sport, I'm not that adept at it, and I get very, very tired of listening to men boast about their prowess with a titanium-shafted stick.

So when this particular man asked me what I liked to drink and then bought me a thousand-dollar bottle of bubbly, I was not an unhappy girl. At this point in my existence, I love a guy who doesn't think twice about throwing out a bit of green on a gal. I used to consider it showy but now that the realities of single parenthood have hit, I find a date's propensity for financial generosity to be a large plus in the *man* column. He also had big strong arms and a warm body, and was a good kisser and a good cuddler. Doc Johnson had none of those attributes.

The man expressed a desire to please me. Another big check in the asset column. We used protection, which, in a way, felt a lot like Doc Johnson, and while the sex lacked the precision and pleasure of the good doctor, I had no real complaints. I didn't have to clean him, or put him away, or worry—God forbid—that my children would find him hidden in the closet. But this fine gentleman had one major drawback: He snored. I mean, serious, big-time logsawing. This is never a worry with Doc Johnson. Even if I'm too tired to put him away, he takes up practically no room and, as long as he's not in motion, makes no noise.

Then there's the morning-after bad-breath thing and overall awkwardness of finding yourself in bed with someone you don't really know, but I didn't have much of that with this man. We actually shared a sweet moment before I announced that it was time for me to make my exit. He was adamant about wanting to spend more time with me and not having this be a one-night stand. That was an ego boost of rather major proportion and something that only a real red-blooded human being can give.

The knowledge that I was still attractive and interesting to a man who I thought was both those things . . . well, that gave me a spark for quite some time. He was extremely attentive the next time we met (which was later that day) and continued to show interest for several months after that even though we lived in different cities and were captive to crazy schedules. The friendship fizzled, but that was because of our different lifestyles and philosophies. So much for man.

Now for machine.

Okay, so I joke all the time about how much easier it is to have a relationship with someone who needs only batteries to function. Truthfully, during this time of transition in my life, when everything is kind of complicated, it's been nice to have something simple, something with no strings attached, something that's perfectly on target and exists for the sole purpose of pleasing me. But do I prefer machine to man? Of course not. I can't laugh with my faux friend, can't dance, smooch, hide under the comforter, or discuss why I think George W. is a bonehead and why I wish Martin Sheen were the real president. I miss warmth and caring and having the eyes of someone across from me look like they're actually happy to be right where they are.

But life, at least my life, has not proven to be anywhere near a Tom Hanks–Meg Ryan romantic comedy, so while I'm living the journey and washing the dishes and making sure I sign the homework folder, I'm grateful for Doc Johnson, who can take care of me in my moments of need and who doesn't care what I look like, what I weigh, or if I've worn the same T-shirt to bed three nights in row. He doesn't notice that once a month there's a zit the size of the Chrysler Building on my chin. Heck, he's even good when the batteries start to get a little low.

In my darker moments, I worry if I will ever be as happy with someone who doesn't vibrate. But that usually passes. I'm just happy that in lieu of getting what I want in the flesh, I've got what I need in silicon. Not that Doc Johnson will help me to manage, in any way, a relationship that is both sexual and emotional. There is, after all, no emotional learning curve with my battery-operated boy. There is no emotion, period. And sometimes that's the real beauty of him.

ME TALK DIRTY ONE DAY
by Sarah Mahoney

 Some forty-something women owe their sexual re-awakenings to *Cosmo* or *Sex and the City* reruns. Me? I have Uncle Sam and Saddam Hussein to thank for my discovery of phone sex and the power of my lover's voice.

Believe me, I am grateful; I had always thought of myself as someone who was lucky to be having any sex, let alone good sex. Then I found a great boyfriend, and sex with him was more than wonderful, like ice cream with sprinkles and syrup. But once we started talking on the phone, I saw lovemaking in a whole new way. Not like dessert; not even like our daily bread. I realized that sex, very simply, was what held us together, and that finally I was part of a couple that would find a way to have it, no matter what.

It wasn't that long ago that I was a magazine editor and

divorced mother of two living a lunatic's life in New York. I juggled temperamental writers and celebrity covers with PTA meetings and teacher's conferences. On the odd—very odd—Saturday night, I'd go out on a date. A few of those brief encounters fought their way to becoming short relationships, which mostly consisted of canceled and rescheduled dinners and talking about how tired we were. Like many women I knew, I needed naps and triple-shot lattes way more than I needed sex.

So I made some big changes. Quit my job and had a garage sale, trading in a tiny brick town house in Queens for life in rural Maine. It occurred to me that a cow town of two thousand wouldn't offer much in the way of a social life, but having spent five years in the wilderness of New York dating, I had to ask myself: Could it be any worse?

That it could be so much better never crossed my mind, but less than a year later, when I was out with some new friends listening to music, the man of my dreams asked me to dance. Since I'd been doing more sitting than dancing, a T-shirt slogan that could sum up my life, I said yes. We danced and chatted, finding some common ground: He liked Bonnie Raitt, and so did I. His three kids were roughly the same ages as my two. But after years of listening to hyperanalytical New York professionals, I found dazzling differences as well. Dennis drove a pickup, hunted deer, loved country music, and never talked about red and blue states. And even more stunning, he was a full-time soldier, stationed nearby.

People say timing is everything in new relationships, and ours was particularly bad. We met February 8, 2003, and while the invasion of Iraq wouldn't technically begin for another month or so, we all knew it was coming. A few days after we met, my dream man called and said, "The good news is I can still have dinner with you. The bad news is that my unit just went on alert, and I may leave for Iraq soon." The term *on alert* has a very specific military definition: It means that soldiers must have their bags packed and their wills written and be ready to report to their base within twenty-four hours. A voice inside my head kept whispering, "You must be *nuts* going out with this guy."

The war started, and each day I watched CNN looking for omens with the selfish and myopic eye of a woman who had been single too long. I was glued to the embedded journalists' reports from the front, to Donald Rumsfeld's predictions, and to the home movies from al-Qaeda. We continued to date, tentatively and timidly, fully expecting Dennis to be whisked away within weeks if not days. Units all around us deployed, but somehow, his stayed put. In less than a month, the war ended. And while the large number of soldiers stationed in Iraq still dominated the news, the urgency of it all began to fade.

I let my guard down, and so did Dennis. By Easter, he'd taken me fishing in the White Mountains. By Memorial Day, he'd taken my kids and me camping, teaching them how to build a fire and stop the dogs from knocking the tent down. He bought a chain saw and cut down a few dozen trees for me, then rented an excavator and dug up the stumps. This was true romance, Maine style, and I fell in love.

One Sunday morning in late November, Dennis was frying bacon in my kitchen when the phone rang. I answered, and it was his commanding officer. We both knew why he'd get that call on a weekend; he was going to Iraq, and soon. He shipped out to Fort Drum before Christmas, and by early February—a year after we'd met—he was writing me long love letters from a twelve-man tent in southern Iraq.

I was surprised at how quickly he and I settled into a peaceful wartime routine. Luck was constantly with us. Because he worked in administration in a transportation company, he had steady access to e-mail. And since he worked nights, he had plenty of privacy, sharing the office space with just one other solider, not a whole platoon. Despite the unbelievable expense of international phone cards, those sporadic, crackling conversations kept Operation True Romance alive.

The connections were never very good. I'd have to speak and wait a bit, because it took so long for my voice to carry. We learned to say "I love you" right away since so many calls would get cut off, or the phone card would run out. Then we talked about mundane things. How he was, how I was, how the kids were, how the weather was. I bitched about record snowfall and having to shovel all by

myself. He bitched about 120-degree days and the fleabites
on his wrists and ankles. And I'd say plenty of "I'm so glad
you're okay" and "I wish you were home." And we'd both
say "I love you" and "I miss you" a lot. We made kissing
noises into the phone, something I think I had last done in
eighth grade.

One day, though, he surprised me. "What are you wearing? Are you alone?" I was startled. He was putting a long-
distance move on me! I had enough sense, at least, looking
down at the uniform of a freelance writer—stretched-out
yoga pants and a tattered Save the Endangered Mountain
Lynx T-shirt—to know that I should lie. "Purple lace un-
derpants," I said. "Nothing else. And yes, I'm alone."

These were only partial lies. I actually owned purple
lace undies, and Dennis had certainly seen them. "I love
those," he murmured. "What are you doing? Are you
touching yourself?" Before I knew it, we were doing it,
me in my office chair in Maine in front of two curious
dogs, and him in an office chair in the cradle of civiliza-
tion, praying that another soldier wouldn't walk in. It
was great.

I thought about it for days after and wondered how
something so impersonal could make me feel so close to
him and be quite that orgasmic. After all, it was just me
and the same fingers I've been using since, well, birth—
and quite frequently since Dennis deployed. What I didn't
count on was just how sexy his voice was. It wasn't that he
said anything new or different. In fact, it was the opposite;

he said and made the same noises as if we were having sex right here at home. It was like an audio scrapbook of our greatest hits.

We kept it up, and he was able to call every few weeks. Sometimes, he'd send me a heads-up e-mail beforehand. I liked being able to dress up for his phone calls; I'd even shave my legs. There were plenty of times he couldn't call. He and his partner were responsible for keeping track of dozens of the unit's trucks as they traveled around Iraq or down into Kuwait for supplies. Sometimes they'd take fire from insurgents, hit roadside bombs, or just break down. Clearly, sweaty phone calls had to take a backseat.

We got good at it. In phone sex, just like in real life, simultaneous orgasms are rare. But phone sex got me off about 50 percent faster than Dennis. I was finally getting a lesson in being the first one to the finish line. I'd keep talking until he was done, and then we'd keep whispering for a few minutes, the spoken-word version of spooning.

One day, it all turned ugly. "That was so great that I don't care who heard us," he announced after finishing. "Who would hear us?" I asked, in complete innocence.

"These calls are monitored," he explained. "They have to be. For security." A world away, I sat in horrified silence, sheepishly pulling up my yoga pants. Dennis could tell he was about to get cut back to "How is the weather there?" phone calls, and he started backpedaling as fast as he could.

"Military intelligence has to randomly monitor all kinds

of communications, not every e-mail and every phone call. But they have to check," he explained.

I was still mute.

"Imagine if a soldier were to call home and say he was heading to Kirkuk on a mission on Thursday—that would give enemies advance information about troop movements. That would be dangerous, right?"

I remained silent.

"I'm sure they don't listen to entire phone conversations," he said. Even with the time delay, I could hear the pleading edge in his voice.

In my mind, I was fending off images of twenty-year-old specialists with crew cuts, leering in their headphones and saying, "Hey, everybody, check this one out!" I imagined them accosting Dennis in the chow line, playfully punching him in the arm the next day at lunch.

"Do you know them? Are they guys in your unit?" While I didn't know many of the people in his company, I had gotten to know a few wives, back at the Christmas cookie party. Had I just copulated in full earshot of some of their husbands? I felt like . . . a middle-aged Paris Hilton. Someone my age should know better.

He explained that no, they weren't in his unit, and he didn't know them. But yes, they were stationed in the same camp and walked by one another all day. "I'm sorry," I said. "I can't do this anymore."

And for a few weeks, we didn't.

But he called one day when he was alone in the office.

I'd had a long, rough day and was really missing him. He started whispering, and I started rationalizing. "You know," I said, "they probably intercept a lot of these calls."

"Um-hmm," Dennis whispered.

"And it's not like I'm ever going to meet any of these guys at a barbecue or anything."

"Um-hmm," Dennis whispered.

"Besides," I said, "I bet we could ask anybody—Colin Powell, Donald Rumsfeld. I bet General Eisenhower would have had phone sex if he could have. It's not like what we're doing is wrong—we miss each other." I thought about how hard it is for soldiers like Dennis to leave behind wives or girlfriends, kids and families, to live in muddy tents for months at a time, risking their lives, watching the same DVDs, and fantasizing about a cup of real coffee. Is a little phone sex so very different than writing a love letter or sending care packages full of trail mix, Vienna sausages, and *Men's Health*? Hell, I was practically doing my patriotic duty: SUPPORT OUR TROOPS.

Dennis whispered some more and started talking about all the ways he would touch me if I were tucked in his sleeping bag with him, about all the ways I would touch him. At first, it was hard to concentrate, and I kept wondering who might be listening. I pictured Radar from *M*A*S*H*. But after a minute or two, I stopped thinking about Radar, and let Dennis's voice drown out everything else. God help me, I thought when we were done. Now I'm an exhibitionist, too.

And so we hummed through his fourteen-month tour. He came home for two weeks in July and proposed on the back porch. Then he came home on Valentine's Day for good, and we married not long afterward. We settled down into our sexual routine, with one huge difference: Almost every time, Dennis started by whispering in my ear. He'd tell me what he was going to do to me, and then he'd do it. And I'd talk back. Sometimes, we'd just deliver the play-by-play, but sometimes, we'd push the envelope, experimenting with dirtier words, or with orders instead of requests.

"We talk all the time now," I said to him one night. "It's different."

"Better different?" he asked.

"Definitely," I said.

"Then we should do more things that are different."

And thus Friday, formerly known as Pizza Night because we sent my kids off to their father's (yes, he relocated to Maine, too) with bellies full of pepperoni, has become Something Different Night. After the kids leave, my husband and I eat grown-up food and have creative sex. Since it began, Something Different Night has involved ice cream, pillows, lingerie, and new positions—yoga-inspired, from *Glamour,* and a memorable one called dash-boarding, from *Maxim.* Some of our ideas have been very successful. Some have fallen flat. I didn't like it when he talked in cartoon voices; he was pretty underwhelmed by my makeshift handcuffs. Some, like the time he spanked me in the middle of sex, have actually made us laugh so hard that we've fallen off the bed, losing all desire (and ability) to finish what we started.

I don't know how long we'll be able to keep these Friday-night specials coming. But I do know one thing: I'll have Dennis keep whispering all through them, rubbing his chin stubble on my neck as he does. Whether it's long-distance from Iraq or right beside me, what now makes our lovemaking sexy is the sound of his voice. Not that sex was bad before, any more than silent movies are worse than talkies. But like Hollywood directors, I discovered that a sound track is transformational.

BETTER LATE THAN NEVER
by Michael Corcoran

The idea that I might, at age forty-one, be looking in the rearview mirror at my sex life and trying to put it into a context that you might expect from someone of my age—well, it's a very difficult thing for me to do. Not because I'm squeamish about the subject, or prudish, or anything of the sort. In fact, I'm much, much more fond of sex than any of the nuns who taught me in grade school would care to know, and I'm not embarrassed to talk about the topic in general or about its place in my life now or then or whenever. However, for me to put my sex life into perspective requires me to put my entire life under the microscope, and that, as we all know, is a most unsettling thing to do.

To many of you, sex and the rest of your life seem linked, but in my case they actually are forever and irrevocably joined at the, er, pelvis—the Siamese twins of my existence. By modern standards, I grew up in a big family, the youngest of six children—four brothers and a sister. You've no doubt guessed from that tiny bit of information that we were raised Catholic, and that my bloodlines are primarily Irish (although my mom's father was born in Poland, leaving me a love/hate relationship with kielbasa to go along with my other quirks. My family loves it, I hate it, especially the sight of the fat globules it leaves floating in a pot of water after it has been boiled, something my father and I used to jokingly refer to as *kielbas-ier,* a play on the name of the cognac Courvoisier).

When I reached the age where my sex drive achieved Mach speed, I knew next to nothing about sex, and what I did know was worthless. I knew, for example, that one of the priests in my parish school could draw a grotesque rendering of a penis on the blackboard and then explain in a stultifying monotone that it somehow did God's work of procreation. I also knew, thanks to my adroitness at uncovering my brothers' secretly stashed magazines, that everyone who wrote in to *Penthouse* couldn't believe what had happened to them almost as much as they couldn't believe they were writing a letter. And that was pretty much it.

There were no birds-and-bees talks from my parents—my dad was my idol, but even in later years I noticed he was terribly uncomfortable when other guys told bawdy jokes around him. My mother was forever concerned with my spiritual well-being and probably earnestly believed that knowledge of sex—let alone having it—was something I shouldn't worry about until after I was married (and she could reasonably base her belief on the fact that I knew premarital sex was a sin. It may have been thought of as such, I can't recall, but I knew it was a bad thing in the eyes of the Church), and, frankly, it wasn't her job to make sure I was well educated in this subject. Maybe they figured I'd pick up what I needed to know along the way, or from my brothers, or maybe they talked about talking about it with me and just never got around to it because they were always tired from raising a big family, or maybe the timing just never seemed right. Whatever the case, I knew nothing about sex through most of my high school years, other than what I heard guys talking about, and I was inclined then (as I am now when I hear guys talking about sex) to think that they were mostly full of shit.

Looking at old photos of me from those years, I don't think I look particularly mature, but I must have carried myself older than most seventeen-year-olds. That's the only thing that could have made it possible for me to walk into any place I wanted to and buy beer without being asked for ID. And what does that have to do with my sex life? you ask. Plenty. See, I wasn't a stud athlete and was reticent about talking to people I didn't know (still am), so I didn't know any girls. But one night I went to my buddy Greg's house, and his sister was there with some of her friends. I arrived with the beer, because that was my role. The girls were all pretty, and a few weeks later they asked me if I could get them beer for a party they were having. Sure, I said, and at that party I learned for the first time what jealousy felt like when I saw one of them, a lovely dark-haired girl named Angela, making out with some tool from the football team. In the ensuing few months, I saw that group of girls fairly regularly and eventually worked up the nerve to kiss Angela—the very first kiss of my life.

The two of us became inseparable, and, as it turned out, if you added up what we both knew about sex, it equaled zero. Not that we were wearing out the shock absorbers in the car or anything—we were both Catholic and both terrified we'd go to hell or get caught, so there was no sex for a long time. When we finally did start to move beyond awkward groping and kissing, our sexual ignorance caught up to us. We were married when I was barely twenty. Angela was just nineteen, and four months pregnant with our first child.

So it was sex, or the lack of knowledge regarding it, that set the course of my entire adult existence, hand in hand with Angela's. Whatever brief period of passion we had ended with the conception of our first child. By the time I was twenty-five we had three kids, and I can say in retrospect that I have no idea what we were thinking. What I can tell you for certain is that after the third child was born we weren't much interested in sex. There were little kids to take care of, of course, and jobs, and, entirely on my part, a gradual turning inward and saying, "I've completely messed up my life and there's nothing I can do about it." We were very old while we were very young, and that is not a recipe for good sex.

As I write this we are nearing twenty-one years since the day we were married, and it would be a lie to say it hasn't been a struggle to hold our relationship together. Like most couples who marry too young, we learned we really didn't know each other, that our brains functioned on two entirely different planes, that our expectations of life were vastly different. For my part, at least, there was always a feeling that I'd cheated myself out of all the great sex guys have before they get married, and a lot of the other fun they have, too.

As it turns out, however, living life in reverse isn't such a bad thing, and in fact can be quite amusing and very, very good for your sex life. While other people your age are having their first kids and acting as if no one else has ever had to deal with all that entails, you can kick back and rest easy in the knowledge that your kids are now beautiful, happy, polite, nice, off to college or on the way, and that you are still young and full of newfound energy and, hubba-hubba, your wife is still very hot.

That last fact, that Angela is beautiful and sexy, was always a source of frustration for me during the fallow years of our sex life. How can I aptly describe having that so close and yet out of reach? The best part is that now I don't think about how I would describe that anymore, because I don't need to. With the freedom and time that life in reverse has presented us, we've entered an entirely new and fantastic phase of sex that has become central to our relationship. Rather than seeing sex as something to be squeezed in between responsibilities, it is now something we spend loads of time thinking about, talking about, and doing. And, really, who knew it could be so good! Well, perhaps you, but we're just getting the hang of the whole fun part of it all.

Here's what should be an embarrassing anecdote to illustrate: Recently a friend of ours from out of town spent a few days with us in our old three-story house. That the house is old is key, because as such it's nearly soundproof. When you're on the third floor, where our bedroom is, you can't hear what's going on in the rest of the place. So my wife and I didn't see any harm in a middle-of-the-night romp, despite the fact that we had a guest in the house—who would be the wiser? A few weeks later I was having a beer with that friend during a business conference and asked if he'd had a good time while he stayed with us. "I had no idea," he said, "that two people could have sex for so long. Christ, it must have been two hours! What are you, some sort of porn star or something?" I responded the only way I knew how—I burst out laughing.

That I could laugh at my sex life was something I never thought possible during the large part of my life when I was resigned to having boring and infrequent sex. During that time I never believed it would change, despite endless discussions about how important it was to our relationship and endless efforts to try to make it work. The one thing

I learned about infrequent sex is this: When one partner is ready, the other inevitably is not, and that ratchets up the pressure on both. A wrong touch here, a poorly chosen word there, and whatever heat has been generated is lost just as quickly as the new dose of frustration sets in— and trust me, that is *very* quickly. It is very easy for both partners to conclude that it just isn't worth it.

Whereas we used to spend almost all of our time together out of necessity, Angela and I now lead more separate lives. We have an apartment in New York, where I work, and our primary residence is in Pennsylvania. I spend a few nights a week in the city, alone, because it makes my life easier. She pops in for the night occasionally, and I head back to Pennsylvania one night a week and on weekends, and that arrangement has led to another discovery on our part: while the jury is still out on whether absence makes the heart grow fonder, it certainly heats things up in the bedroom when we're together. We make plans to have sex and look forward to it. In some magical way, our being apart has lent to our sex life the one thing that it always lacked: spontaneity.

Just a few weeks ago while we were home in Pennsylvania, my wife suggested to me that we go to a nearby hotel that she'd heard had fireplaces in the rooms. The place was just five miles from our house, a house that has a perfectly good bed and certainly would have been empty of kids later that night. But we didn't want to wait—couldn't wait—so we lied to the two kids still at home, told them we were going to the movies. Instead, we checked into that hotel and had sex—over and over again—for hours. We shared the strangely exciting feeling that we were doing something illicit, and that in turn led to some super-hot sex that left us exhausted and fulfilled, not to mention wondering about what movie we'd lie about having seen, and how come we couldn't really explain what happened in it. ("Really, son, you might want to see it yourself, and I'd hate to ruin it for you.")

You may find it a bit odd that I haven't made a single reference to love up to this point, and you may think that I'm just some typical guy who, like most typical guys, is capable of separating sex from love, doesn't feel it necessary for there to be a connection between the two. To some degree you'd be correct—I'm capable of keeping the two things distanced in my mind, but I don't. Or more to the point, I don't know how.

It's not possible to go through all the years and challenges that my wife and I have without love being all around and part of everything. The sex, the fights, the deaths, the kids, the money problems, the changes inside our heads, the moving all over the country, the sex, all of that is infused with love. So sex, to me at least, is another part of life—a huge part, a fantastic part, and a necessary part—but just a piece of something bigger and more meaningful.

I wouldn't want to live without sex, no sir, I most certainly would not, and I have no desire to go back to the days when we had it anytime we wanted as long as it wasn't Sunday through Saturday. But I do now, from a much more mature perspective than I had when I was nineteen (beer purchases notwithstanding), realize that good and frequent sex is wrapped up in something much bigger, and I've found I'm much happier when I don't sit around thinking about what that something much bigger is. It's life, of course, and I just want to stay busy living it without letting my mind mess it up for me. I almost just wrote *mess it up for me again,* but I realize now, looking back, that I never really messed up my life—in truth, it has been charmed and blessed. I'm just living it in reverse.

SEX AFTER (NEAR) DEATH
by Caroline Leavitt

It's a shimmering sunny day and I'm zipping through Manhattan like a racehorse. I'm forty-three years old, and I swear, even though I know this sounds weird coming from someone as insecure as I am about my looks, that I look gorgeous. Everyone says that some women glow in pregnancy, but here, in my ninth month, I'm the sun, the stars, and the moon all put together.

I haven't gained any weight except for the beautiful bump that is my belly. My hair is thick and curly and half-way down my back. My skin is luminous and smooth. My breasts are so lush that I sometimes stand naked in front of the mirror just to admire them. My husband, Jeff, comes up behind me to nuzzle my neck, to touch my belly, to tumble me into bed.

"You're the sexiest mama-to-be I've ever seen," a friend tells me, and I laugh because it's true. I've never felt or looked so sexy in my life.

Many women in the last months of pregnancy don't have sex. It's too uncomfortable, too cumbersome. But Jeff is intoxicated with my new shape, and, on my part, every cell of my body seems alive. Quantity of sex isn't changing, but quality sure is. Making love now seems different, more charged. Just a touch now can make me shiver; a breath on my neck gets me tumbling. "You're giving off some sort of hormonal charge that's making me crazy," Jeff swears. He slides a finger down my arm and then stops. "What are we going to do after you have the baby?" he asks, and I know what he means. No sex for six weeks afterward. We'll put a big red *X* on the calendar the same way we did after my miscarriage. We'll wait it out. Jeff brushes back my hair and kisses me. "What's six weeks?" Jeff says, and then his face tightens into a stricken look and we burst out laughing. We laugh at the people who say, "What do you call people who don't have sex?" The answer? "Parents."

"We'll never be like that," Jeff says.

My labor was easy. Though I had a C-section, I was awake for the procedure and it was incredible; Max, my son, was like moonlight, perfect and amazing, and I was so flooded with happiness, I was grabbing nurses. "Did you see how beautiful my son is?" I asked. The nip of Max's mouth on my breast was sensual. The smell of his creamy skin intoxicating. I wanted to tell Jeff. I wanted to tell him

in bed when we were naked. The next day, while many of
the vaginal-birth mothers were sleeping, I was walking the
halls, eager to go home.

Three days later, I was in a coma. I found out later that
none of the doctors expected me to survive and that all
my family was called to stand watch. But five emergency
operations, one near death, and two months later, I came
home to a yearlong recuperation.

What I had was rare and deadly, a one-in-a-million
glitch in my immune system called postpartum factor VIII
inhibitor. Your body doesn't recognize your blood-clotting
factors anymore, and so it merrily begins to destroy them.
You bleed. From anywhere. Eyes, brain, major organs. In
the end it turned out I was lucky I had had a C-section, because most of my bleeding was where I had been cut—my
uterus and my stomach muscles. To stop a lot of the bleeding, they did an emergency hysterectomy. And when I kept
bleeding, it was from an adjoining muscle on my left side.
Right where Max, my baby, loved to roost when I was
pregnant with him.

I swam on morphine in the hospital. I woke up to find
doctors around me, watching me, frowning. "Do you
know where you are?" one asked as I struggled to get up
and found I couldn't move. "My husband and baby are
dead, aren't they," I said, and then, before they could answer, I fell down into blackness. I woke the next time to lift
up the sheets and find, to my horror, four clear plastic vials
filling with blood attached to a seam in my belly.

Gradually, they lowered the meds. I knew where I was. I knew my husband and child were alive, but I couldn't be with them. "When can I see my baby?" I asked. I was horrified because I knew how crucial the first months were for bonding. I knew all that I was missing.

"Too many diseases in a hospital for a little baby," a doctor told me. "When you get home, you can see him."

"And when will that be?" I cried, but the doctor glided out of the room.

Worse, I couldn't seem to move. When can I walk? I kept asking the nurses, and the way they exchanged glances didn't exactly fill my heart with hope. "Wait," they said. "Be patient."

My hematologist was a German woman with a thick accent. No-nonsense, she strode in with a clipboard, sat down, and said, "Well. I will talk first, and then you will ask questions." I listened, still hazy on medication. She wanted me to stay in the hospital another month. I had had more than one hundred blood transfusions, so I had to be tested for AIDS and hepatitis. "Just a precaution," she said.

"What about my baby? When can I see him?"

"The baby is fine," she said. "Your big worry is not the baby. It's bleeding. In the hospital, we can try to stop it."

Try. She said *try.* "What if you can't stop the bleeding? Could I bleed to death?"

"Why, of course," she said, "and from any organ," and when I burst into tears, she pushed out a breath. "Well, you *asked*," she snapped. She started ticking off what I couldn't do. I couldn't hold my son because I might start to bleed internally. I couldn't walk because I might bleed. I couldn't eat anything that was too hard because I might bleed. And I had to be really careful going to the bathroom. I looked at her, astonished.

"But of course, you have to try to do these things or your muscles will atrophy," she said. "We'll just keep close watch, take it in baby steps."

I thought about not listening, about getting up and walking out of the hospital and running home to Jeff and my son. I thought about what it would feel like to hold my baby. And I thought about being held by Jeff, about having a normal, happy family life.

"What about sex?" I said.

"Now?" She raised one brow. "You're in the hospital."

"Later, when I get out."

Two nurses came into the room. One had my medicine cups, eight of them on a tray. The other carried a pitcher.

"No sex," said the doctor crisply. "Not for six months to a year."

I heard one of the nurses take in her breath, saw them exchange glances.

"None at all?" I said.

She shook her head.

"Anytime you move, you could induce a bleed that we can't stop. There's too much muscle activity in sex to risk it."

"What about oral sex?" I persisted.

She shook her head and leaned closer.

"What about touching?"

"I don't even want you to dream of having an orgasm," she told me.

When the hematologist left, I curled into a ball. That day, when someone came to take blood (which happened every four hours), I screamed, "Get the fuck away from me!"

"I have to take your blood," he said quietly, and I screamed again, so loudly the nurse came in, the same one who had heard the no-sex.

"Do it later," she told him quietly.

When I told Jeff about the no-sex, I was crying, but he just sat beside me and held my hand. "So we'll wait," he said. "It doesn't matter. All that matters is you're alive and you're coming home."

Two months later, I could walk a little, though I had a wheelchair. I came home to a stranger: a tiny little baby I couldn't hold, who I swore drew away when he saw me. And to a husband I couldn't have sex with. Maybe I was the stranger to them—someone disengaged who couldn't hug either one of them, who had to blow kisses like a debutante as she glided past.

My body was mapped with surgical scars in all directions. The biggest, a seam across my belly, kept opening up, so I wore layers upon layers of gauze that had to be wrapped and taped about my body and changed every few hours when they soaked through. The whole shape of my belly was strange, a triangle with a peak.

"You're going to have to live with that shape," my hematologist had told me. "No one wants to do any unnecessary surgery on you to repair it." When she saw my face, she shook her head. "So you won't wear a bikini, so what?" I blinked at her and pulled the sheets up to my chin.

This is what I still couldn't do. I couldn't pick up my brand-new baby, who warmed more to the baby nurse than to me. I couldn't use a knife. I couldn't bite my nails. I couldn't climb more than two steps, though I had to at least try to do two every day. I had to watch out for accidents or falls. I couldn't get up too quickly.

And I couldn't have sex.

Did I even feel like it? The truth was no, I did not. My sexual feelings seemed dormant. I was in pain or woozy or nauseated or all three. It hurt to be touched, and every time someone did touch me, I was terrified I would bruise and then bleed and wind up back in the hospital. Plus, I hated my body, so why would I want it to be touched? But what I did want was the *idea* of sex, the connection and the release.

Just putting on a clean shirt in the morning made me wince. Just climbing one step made me as terrified as I was elated, because even though I had been strong enough to do it, who knew if it had triggered a bleed? I looked at Jeff, fresh from the shower, in a new black T-shirt, holding our son, and I wanted more than anything to feel his breath quicken when he touched me. I was desperate for the everydayness of it, the feeling that we were a husband and wife, and lovemaking was as natural to us as sitting down to breakfast. And I couldn't have it. I was an alien on a family planet, and physical intimacy was for humans, not for me. Would I ever be a sexual being again?

I was cranky and depressed and jealous of the baby nurse who brought Max in to say hello and then whisked him away because I had to stay in bed. I didn't sleep at night. I was terrified I'd wake and find Jeff on the couch, with an excuse—that he wanted me to rest, that he had done it for me—but I would know that really, he had done it for him, because it was too hard to look at me. All day I watched him, trying to see if he was looking at me as if I were a freak, which was exactly what I thought. "I look horrible," I said, but I really meant, I am a freak.

"You look gorgeous to me," he said, and I thought what he really means is, Yes, you are a freak, but I'm stuck with you.

～

It's six months later and my hematologist smiled at me. "All right, you can have sex now. But you be gentle."

Instead of being happy, I was terrified. I didn't feel like a sexual being anymore. I slept in T-shirts and layers of gauze and I couldn't imagine the undertow of passion ever being able to pull me under.

But we planned. We had music and candles, but I might as well have been a box of hammers for all the feeling I had. I didn't feel the usual pulse of desire. I didn't feel attractive or sexy or anything. I wanted the lights out, the covers over me. I had bought a new nightgown for the occasion, a simple silky white with tiny little straps, but I felt big and cumbersome in it, as sexy as my grandmother.

"You okay?" Jeff asked quietly. "Do you not want to do this? It's okay if you need to stop, you know."

"Of course I want to do this," I said, and it wasn't totally a lie. I wanted the sexual part of our life back, I wanted the sexual part of me to come out of remission. And if this wasn't wild passion for me, well, it was a start, something necessary that had to be done.

When Jeff touched me, my first instinct was to curl up into a ball. Tightly wound, I tried to smooth my breathing. "Let go," I told myself, and I had a sudden, terrifying image, the elevator door in Kubrick's movie *The Shining*, the scene where blood is pouring through the door, until it covers the screen. I sucked in my breath. Jeff touched part of my belly. They had cut nerves and I couldn't feel anything. "That feel good?" Jeff murmured encouragingly. I didn't know how to answer so I let him keep touching me.

The sensation in that part of my body would never come back, but maybe the desire for sex would.

Afterward, he held me, and we fell asleep like that. My eyes were open in the dark. It's a start, I told myself. A start.

One day, I was playing with Max when he reached up and grabbed a hank of my hair. To both our surprise, it came off in his hand, and we both began to cry. If having a chewed-up belly wasn't enough to make me want to lock myself away, now my head grew patchy and bald. My skin was turning gray and my face was becoming a moon. Worse, my body was bloating so I looked a hundred pounds heavier than I was, though I wasn't eating. "Oh, that's just the steroids," my doctor said. She frowned, glancing at the reports of my blood counts. "I think we may want to try chemo to get the inhibitor down. I don't like these numbers." She shuffled the papers. "Or maybe not. We will wait and we will see."

Chemo. I would lose more hair. I would look worse. I would feel sicker.

And I would want sex even less.

A week passed and then another. With all my medical expenses, we were hurting for money, and when I got a call from Kate, a woman I used to work with, offering me freelance work writing a catalog for Victoria's Secret, I knew I couldn't turn it down. Plus working would make me feel more normal. "Messenger it," I said.

"Can you come in instead?" Kate said. "I need to show you the merchandise."

I hesitated. I was a novelist but I did freelance fashion work, and I knew the routine. As a novelist I could write in my pajamas and sneakers if I wanted, but for fashion writing, I had to look the part. I had a closetful of tight little skirts and expensive fitted sweaters, but I could no more fit in them now than I could fit in a bikini.

"I've been sick," I blurted. "I look really different."

"Come on, you always look great," Kate said. "I remember that little suede dress you had, how I coveted it! And those vintage cashmeres! You want the job? Come on in and get it."

It was the first work I had done in months. I was walking then, and if I was careful, it would be safe for me to take the subway.

I had done the best I could that day. Because of my belly and all the gauze, I couldn't wear a tight skirt. I wore a muumuu of a dress and black tights, and I still looked hugely pregnant. My hair had turned gray and I tried to tie what was left of it into a scrubby little tail in back. I swept blush on my gray cheeks, put on lipstick and mascara, but still, staring at myself in the mirror, I could see something was wrong.

The subway lurched to a stop. Three teenage girls got on, and when they saw me, they visibly stared, and I flushed. One began whispering to the other, and I was too exhausted to fight, to do anything. Let them stare. I walked to the Victoria's Secret office, and out sprang Kate, thin and lithe and beautiful with a magnificent sweep of blond hair, and when she saw me, she faltered.

"Well," she said crisply, "let's talk about your assignment." She talked but I couldn't listen. I kept looking at her flat stomach while my dress billowed around me. At the lushness of her hair, while mine was pulled back into one little tail. I wanted to shake her. But she kept talking. And after that day, she never gave me any work again.

It took a year for me to get better. Jeff gave me and Max time to be together, to get to know each other. I couldn't breast-feed, but I could hold him finally, against me, and the feel of him against me made me burst into tears. And then, one day, while trying to arrange what hair I had left, I felt a tuft. A curl of hair! I marked my calendar for when I would start looking more normal. For when I might feel something other than exhaustion.

Sex was still more a badge of being normal than a feeling of anything. But gradually, I had to make the leap, to let go, to trust that I wouldn't hemorrhage, that it wouldn't hurt, that I would feel again like a normal person. "Sex is overrated," said one of my friends, when we were having lunch one day. "It's for women in their twenties, not us old warhorses."

I looked at her askance. I felt the breeze ruffling through my hair. That day, I had gone, weeping, to the woman who cut my hair. She boosted the color so it was blue-black, she cut it into a curly cap about my head so it looked lush and thick. My skin was pink again, and even my belly was beginning to go down.

"Give me hugs and comfort anytime," my friend continued. "That's all women our age want. Fuck sex."

When I left lunch, I called Jeff. "Tonight," I whispered. "Let's try tonight."

I walked home. I remembered how when we had first started dating, we couldn't get enough of each other. I was working at Macy's then, writing fashion copy freelance while writing my novel at home, and I'd tell my boss I didn't feel well and then I'd call Jeff on my cell phone. "Come over," I said, my voice husky. As soon as he came through the door, we'd be unbuttoning each other, sliding off clothes, tumbling.

I suddenly realized, to my delight, that just thinking about it was making me flush.

When I got to our house, my key fumbled in the lock because I was so excited that I was excited. The door was half open, and there was Jeff. He grabbed both my hands. He pulled me through the door.

This time, I was the one unbuttoning my shirt and then his. I felt a strange new heat forming in my stomach, moving up my body. While I was ill, I often got dizzy, but this time, I was dizzy from desire. Jeff drew himself down to my belly and he kissed one of my scars, the biggest one. It was sexual, but it was also the deepest kind of affirmation of what we'd been through together, what we, what our marriage, had survived. Instead of flinching, I pulled my pants down lower. I yanked off my panties. I thought words like *torrid* and *passionate*, and then we were on the floor, and finally, blissfully, I stopped thinking altogether.

UNLEASH THE BEAST

by Josephine Thomas
(pseud.)

〰 I am faithful to my husband for 2,292 days. But on the 2,293rd day, I have hormonal teenage sex with a veritable stranger in his divorced-bachelor pad by the train tracks. I've slept with some sixty men over two decades and yet it's with this middle-aged man—graying, with wrinkles and soft muscles—that I truly discover sex.

He is a stranger, but we have a history. One day two years ago, we sat next to each other on the commuter bus, chatting, flirting. I found him incredibly sexy. Our thighs touched in a way that suggested it wasn't a coincidence. I fantasized about him a good deal in the following weeks. I imagined that, engrossed in conversation, I'd miss my stop, and he'd offer, like a gentleman, to drive me home once we got to his place. Of course we'd have incredibly hot, animalistic sex on his enclosed sunporch, and there'd be nothing gentlemanly about it.

Now, all this time later, I am waiting one morning for the commuter train when I see him walk onto the platform. He comes straight over to me, smiling broadly, as if we're old friends. He's just come from the chiropractor because he hurt his back. He looks good. He remembers my name. I learn within minutes that he's separated from his wife and is living a couple blocks away. He neglects to mention that he has a steady girlfriend because, consciously or not, he knows what I know: We're going to fuck. Soon.

The fact that I don't feel one ounce guilty about contemplating adultery should make me feel like a coldhearted sociopath, but it doesn't. The plain truth is that I've had a problem with fidelity all my romantic life. I was never faithful to any of my boyfriends. I would cheat on current boyfriends with new ones, on new ones with exes. I once left a lover in my bed for a dalliance with another, then came back as if I'd just run down to the store for milk. In fact, infidelity is a pastime of which I am rather fond, a behavior that I tamped down when I exchanged vows with my husband but that I never truly buried.

The moment I see train-station man, with his impish grin, I am instantly my good old, bad old self again. Maybe it's because he shows up after a long, tedious spell of monogamy. Maybe it's because childbirth deeply wounded my body image, and his flattery is just the balm to soothe it. It's also possible that I'm more resentful than I realize of my husband, who refuses to take a turn getting up early with the kids on weekends because he's so tired from doing the very important job that pays for our really nice house. Whatever the reason, train-station man manages not only to revive my mischievous, affair-loving streak, but ultimately to open me up to something that is, oddly enough, new to me: the exquisite joy of sex.

His first e-mail, later that day — after the train doesn't show and he gives me a lift into the city — is fairly innocent but suggestive enough if I choose to take the bait:

> *What a treat to see you waiting for the train this morning. I thought it would be nice to talk to you for a few minutes before it arrived. Little did I know I would get to have you all to myself for an entire car ride into the city. Now I'm glad I hurt my back. :)*

I feel no shame or fear in pursuing this, only pure adrenaline-pumped pleasure. I know exactly where it's going to lead because that's where I want it to lead. I admit in my reply to him that I wasn't able to concentrate much at my meeting since my mind was "elsewhere." This time he takes the bait and writes back:

> *I remember very well the feeling of sitting so close to you on the bus and the pull you describe. And, to tell you the truth, I thought about it yesterday when we walked to get my car. I imagined asking you to*

come upstairs with me for a minute so I could get something I'd forgotten. You are ahead of me on the stairs and we're making small talk as we walk. The sound of our footsteps and of our breathing is echoing slightly in the hallway, but otherwise the building is quiet. Most everyone has gone to work already.

As we start up the last flight before my door, you stop and turn toward me to make a joke about something I just said. I don't stop, though. I keep walking until I'm on the step below you. You pause for a second because I'm standing so close, and the atmosphere changes. Suddenly things are very electric, and the sound of our breathing is now quite pronounced.

My right hand is on the banister, but my left slides up the wall and comes to rest, very lightly, on your hip. I never take my eyes off yours, but my hand moves slowly around the small of your back and pulls you in a little closer. I lean in and place my lips so that they are almost touching your neck, just below the jawline. You can feel my breath warm against your skin, while my other hand grazes your hip and comes to rest on the back of your other leg, just below the hem of your skirt, and slides slowly up and stops just at the point where it meets your . . .

The e-mails quickly cross the line from PG to R, and then NC-17. They reach such a frenzy that a rendezvous is all but inevitable, and about twenty-four hours later, I am in his apartment, naked, my legs wrapped around his torso, his strong arms guiding my body up and down on his. It's amazing. He's amazing. I haven't felt this alive in years.

It's possible that I've had other great lovers before, but that I was too young to fully appreciate their prowess, or maybe I was too distracted by my ulterior motive—the conquest itself—to relax and enjoy. Or maybe it's just that train-station man is more experienced and more confident in bed than any man I've ever been with, so he understands what women need. I do know that he's an extremely generous lover, and that he genuinely wants to give—it's not just a ruse to get to intercourse faster.

Even if the sex weren't stellar, which it is, the ego trip is out of this world.

Here I am, approaching forty. I've had two kids, one by C-section, with a nasty scar to prove it. My breasts have fallen, my hips have widened; I've got grandma arms and saddlebags. And yet here is this very attractive man, well into his forties, beholding my naked body in wonderment as if I'm a Victoria's Secret model, no, make that the Botticelli *Venus* herself, landed on his futon, a gift from heaven. His hands trace the curves up and down my body. He tells me I'm an incredibly tasty thing, hot and sexy and interesting and compelling. I'm addicted.

⌒⌒⌒

Why don't I feel guilty? In part, I blame my upbringing. The daughter of a very public figure, I always seemed exempt from the rules everyone else had to follow. My parents, overachievers themselves and dead set on impressing the world, encouraged me to take shortcuts, to use connections to get things first or more easily, cheaper or faster. If I did the conventional thing, if I actually filled out a job or school application and sent it off cold to an anonymous person, or walked into a store and bought something retail, I was not being clever, not using every resource to my advantage. And nothing succeeded like success. The message was clear: Achieve your goal. The subtext was even clearer: Whatever it takes. With each success, I lapped up my parents' praise and then got greedy for more.

Somehow that need for praise and attention translated into sexual conquest. I found, well before puberty, that getting boys to notice me provided the same gratification. By age fourteen, I was a raging slut, seducing boys at school, at camp, in the neighborhood. Every encounter left me high. It was like crack.

For many years I believed I had an insatiable appetite for sex, but whenever I was in a committed relationship, it lost its appeal almost entirely. No, for me sex was about the invincible power I could wield over the opposite sex. And the more illicit the encounter, the better: in a coatroom, in a kiddie pool, on a stage in a darkened theater after hours. I loved feeling I was getting away with something, getting it first or more easily, cheaper or faster.

I slept with so many men that the only way I can remember them is to go through the alphabet, making allowances for those nameless conquests—bouncer at the Ritz, American University senior at the beach, the DJ who got me an autographed Madonna album. When I finally settled down at age twenty-eight, it wasn't so much that I'd found my sexual match as that I'd found other qualities to value. We played Scrabble and did crossword puzzles together; we liked the same bands. Neither of us ever carried a balance on a credit card. He liked when I cooked for him, he loved how I looked in a miniskirt. We got along swimmingly, effortlessly. He'd had his share of conquests too. I felt understood. I had a best friend. I was happy.

Fast-forward ten years. I'm working from my home in the suburbs to be close to my two kids. I hardly ever see my husband, who's gone for some thirteen hours on weekdays, and I hardly see men other than my husband, let alone sexy ones or, even more unimaginable, sexy ones who undress me with their eyes. I feel old, invisible, practically dead. I hired a fairly attractive exterminator once, but then he cleaned up bat shit in my attic and I lost even my very mild interest. The closest I ever got to flirting now was with the cute fathers who occasionally picked up their kids at my daughter's preschool. And that's when the beast inside me—the one that once fed voraciously off male attention—roused from its hibernation long enough for me to feel a flicker of adrenaline, a pang for my glory days as a wild seductress of men. Then it usually sighed, curled up, and went back to sleep.

Not this time. On this day I allow the beast, ravenous

from years of starvation, to come roaring back to life. I don't even try to quiet it. I send train-station man another e-mail, and it's practically pornographic:

I swear I've been totally WET now for days, just from periodic—okay, nearly constant—thinking about your electrifying sexuality. In fact, I actually think my nether regions are kind of swollen from all the excitement. Is that possible?

He replies:

God, I am so fucking hard thinking about your sweet little body and the things I want to do to it that I can barely concentrate on anything else. I didn't tell you this, but that day on the bus, I was slouched down in my seat (so I could feel like I was closer to you) and I was fantasizing about doing things to you, like fucking you with my fingers, and you would have to keep really quiet so the bus driver wouldn't know.

I know that what I'm doing is wrong, but I know it only on an academic level. Inside, I don't care. I can't care. It feels too good. It feels like home. I feel like *me* again, awash in the euphoria of a new relationship and drunk with the power I'm thrilled to realize I still have. And this time it's not over a pimply teen or a brooding college student but over a fully grown man (who, as such, should know better). I get him to leave work early, to duck out of his son's birthday party, to lie to the people he loves just to see me. It's not that I'm mean. It's that I'm addicted—to the ego boost, certainly, but also, perhaps for the first time, to the sex itself.

After the birth of my second child, I cried the first few times I slept with my husband because I just felt so undesirable, like he was sleeping with me out of pity. Poor fat Josie with a nasty scar and a pouchy belly. He told me, charitably, that he "didn't find me unattractive," but his soft dick proved otherwise. We had sex pretty infrequently after that, occasionally noticing a month or more had passed since our last conjugal visit. The frequency picked up slightly over the following year and a half, but at some point during his pushing and grunting, long after I'd lost any lubrication I was able to achieve, I would count the seconds till it was over. Sex began taking place only in the middle of the night when, half-asleep, my husband would get turned on by our spooning and begin clumsily removing my pajamas. I considered it a new low.

Train-station man, with his alabaster skin and pool blue eyes, changed all that by giving me something I so desperately needed—permission to accept and even embrace my body. He writes:

It was delicious doing all the things to you that I had envisioned beforehand, especially approaching you from all different angles. And take it from me: Your

extremely hot body looks good from any angle. My
personal favorites so far are you on top of me, head
thrown back, eyes closed, riding me; you standing,
hands against the wall, half turned back to look at
me while I put my hands all over you; you lying
naked on your side, back to me, while I stroke and
caress you, then slip my finger slowly inside you.

I keep wanting to come over there and throw
you down on any available surface and take you,
again and again and again . . .

What amazes me most is that this man didn't know me
when I was young and nubile with perky breasts and flat
abs, so that now he might merely be looking past the ravages
of time and childbirth. This man is attracted to the woman I
am now, warts and all. And though his e-mails have slowed
to a trickle and become more perfunctory *(Okay then, see*
you at three), the legacy of the affair remains very much
alive—even affecting the way I take care of myself: I'm shaving my legs more often, applying face masks, actually floss-
ing. I'm wearing makeup most days, even with no plans to
leave the house, and I've joined the gym.

The fourth time I sleep with train-station man, the thrill
is beginning to wear off. He's still amazing in bed, but the
fireworks are gone. We're just two grown-up people enjoying a fine afternoon fuck. And as I descend the three flights

to the parking lot behind his building, I wonder if it will be for the last time.

I also realize it almost doesn't matter. I've already reaped an incredible, unforeseen reward from this affair: Far from detracting from my sex life at home, it has significantly improved it—and, by extension, my relationship with my husband—simply by making me feel desirable again and by showing me how much fun sex can be. This affair has been like a giant "aha" moment that's enriched my life beyond belief. It's as though he has helped me become a citizen of the sexual world, and it's a wonderful place to be.

Will sex with my husband ever trump or even match the magical lovemaking I've been enjoying with train-station man? Probably not. But is it better than it's been in a long time? Absolutely. I feel freer to talk dirty, to guide his hands, to show off my body instead of hiding it under the covers. My newfound confidence has rekindled his desire too, adding more fuel to the sexual fire. Better still, we're doing crossword puzzles again. We're eating dinner together and actually talking—the very things that tamed the sex fiend in me in the first place. Just yesterday he downloaded two CDs' worth of my favorite songs and presented them to me as a gift. We're getting back to being involved in each other's lives in that simple, loving way. And that's a huge dividend from an illicit affair with a gray-haired stranger I met at the train station.

WOMAN ON A MISSION
by Deborah Caldwell

At age forty-one, I was a near virgin. Yeah, I'd had sex—I'd been married for sixteen years and I'd given birth to two children. But my husband was my one and only. And we were getting a divorce.

We'd first crossed paths in 1976, on a November Friday night when our rural Pennsylvania high schools played their annual football rivalry. I was a freshman pom-pom girl; D. was a senior tight end. Photos of us appear in our game program books, each of us smiling determinedly into tabula rasa futures. Seven years later, we met officially at our hometown newspaper and began dating. In 1987, we married, having grown up five miles apart and sharing history, career paths, neuroses, and probably a few genes as well.

Some time around year ten, the marriage began to head south, crumbling under an avalanche of work, demands from children, pressure from an ill-conceived move to Texas, and too much familiarity. Eventually it had to end. So in the summer of 2003, I told him I was leaving, and he didn't dispute the decision.

In the weeks leading to our official separation, D. announced he had signed up for online dating sites, telling me, somewhat proudly, that he was ready to "experiment." I followed suit, leading to the jarring moment one morning as I was wiping Colgate off my mouth in the master bathroom that D. revealed he'd spotted my photo and profile on one of the Web sites. After that, we divvied up the dating sites—I took one and he had all the rest—and vowed not to run into each other online.

I pondered what lay ahead as I surfed the Internet in those last few weeks of marriage. Dating, for sure: I pictured candlelit dinners, holding hands with a puppy-eyed hog-tie across the table. Groping in movie theaters perhaps.

Oops, cut to the sex . . . middle-aged sex, with men I couldn't yet imagine. Terrifying. (And maybe a tiny bit exhilarating). I'd always enjoyed the attention of men, and by the time I was in my midthirties, I would sometimes catch myself thinking that I didn't know anything about where that attention could lead. My looming divorce filled me with sorrow, but it also made me realize—once I could allow myself to think about it—that I needed to know. So

I set myself a goal: I would rack up enough sex partners to become what I considered "normal." I'd always been the good girl who followed the rules and tried to be perfect. Now I was ready to join the human race. I wanted to be a red-blooded American woman—sex and all.

My need to embark on this mission had occurred to me the year before, during a wine-soaked night in New York. I had been at a bar with coworkers who got into a discussion about how many sex partners they'd each had. They went around the table, sometimes proudly and sometimes sheepishly, revealing their numbers—ranging from thirty-something down to five, with most people coming in at around twenty. My turn came and I said, "Less than five."

"Three?" someone asked. Nope. Fewer.

"One?"

I acknowledged that, yes, that figure was correct. Just after the nervous silence, one of my colleagues decided to compliment me, saying, "You're a very special person," as if I had been a chastity belt–wearing Victorian royal holding out for a prince.

And so I had to know what I'd been missing, what I wanted in a man sexually. I needed to know myself as a desirable woman. And I really, really wanted to be like everyone else. My target number of sexual exploits: double digits. Low double digits, okay, the lowest possible double digits. I vowed to be normal enough to be hip without being sleazy.

Let me just say here that my married sex life had been mostly fine. D. and I had met when we were young and, because we were both sensitive souls, had sought shelter in each other from the business of young-adult heartbreak and sexual experimentation. On our first date, he took me to a white-tablecloth restaurant. We split strawberry fondue for dessert, ending the evening feeding each other whipped cream–laden berries. After that, it was only a matter of time before we slept together. Once that happened, I felt bound to him; I finally had a sexual relationship, and I didn't have to worry about it anymore.

At that time, the idea of having sex frightened me. I'd grown up in an intellectually liberal but socially conservative home. I could think and voice most anything I wanted, but acting on impulses was frowned upon. And that implicitly meant sex, along with smoking, drinking, drugs, and having too much fun. As a result, though I knew I was smart and appealing in many ways, I wasn't convinced I was desirable. I had dated a number of boys in high school and college before I met D. But I had never been able to let myself risk a broken heart or—good Lord!—one of those awful fraternity brothers taking potshots at my potentially naked thighs.

My internal conflict was unfolding during the seventies and eighties—at the end of free love and drugs, through the beginning of the AIDS epidemic, and most especially in the era of Cyndi Lauper ("Girls Just Want to Have Fun") and Madonna ("Like a Virgin" and "Express Yourself").

During college, nearly all my friends experimented sexually. I wanted to join them, and I was secretly jealous of the girls who could drink, dance, bounce, wiggle—and then put out in an icky fraternity boy's bed.

I was way too scared and way too insecure.

During the early weeks of my first year of college, the fraternity brothers came around to each freshman girl's dorm room and handed out invitations to what were euphemistically called Freshmen Tea Parties. What they really were was a chance for the older guys to get the young hotties drunk on grain-alcohol punch and then lead them into their dens of iniquity. With the invitation, you received a carnation—red, pink, or white—that you handed to the greeter a few days later when you entered the party. If you got a red one, you were fair game; if you got a white one, you were a dog. Of course I got pink; I was cute all right, but I had equivocation written all over my innocent face. I went to a few of the teas. Each time, I'd sip a drink, try to strut around the dance floor in a sexy, catlike manner—and inevitably attract the dorkiest guy in the room. Never mind that even then I knew the entire freshmen tea concept was horribly sexist; I wanted to be a hottie, and I couldn't pull it off.

Twenty years later, as divorce loomed and D. and I liberated each other into the dating world, I was thrilled, in that way you're thrilled when you stare down from the top of a roller coaster. I went on date number one a few weeks after the official separation. At a bar in a neighboring town, I sat watching as the first suitor ambled toward me. His untucked shirt over T-shirt and jeans was a clue to extra paunch. But he was definitely cute and very gentle with my nervousness. We drank exotic martinis (including a hilariously revolting grape one), then took a long walk in a dark park. He was one of the most interesting men I'd ever met, and we had similar philosophies and interests. He played guitar, rode a motorcycle, traded stocks, knew how to Sheetrock, loved to travel, and was a champion athlete. He reinvigorated my long-dormant artistic and musical talents, allowed me to be adventurous and passionate, and adored my spiritual depth. He was also a suburban daddy with two kids the same ages as mine.

At the end of the second date, man number one kissed me in a thunderstorm while handing me a bouquet of flowers. At the end of date three, we made out on my couch after a day of horseback riding (thrilling and sexy!). That's when I panicked: "What do we do about the sex thing?" I asked, pulling away suddenly. He'd been separated a couple years by that point and was, apparently, a pro at dating. Sweet man that he was, he hugged me and said, "It's nice just like this." I sent him home well kissed, but that's it.

A month later, we made love on a Saturday afternoon after a fall hike spent crunching leaves underfoot and quivering with sexual tension. We trooped into his house, took off our jackets, began to kiss, and before I knew it, he was pulling off my shirt and leading me to his bedroom. I couldn't get enough of him. In fact, every time I got near

him after that, I had the same reaction—chemistry border-
ing on hysteria.

For more than two years, we saw each other on and
off whenever one of us wasn't dating someone else—and
we nearly always groped, then grabbed, then ravaged each
other. Man number one was hothothot, while also managing to be a tremendously comforting friend. But although
he was hothothot, he was also a Wounded Man, still deal-
ing with the demons of his failed marriage. Eventually, I
had to move on.

This first intense relationship was a blessing and a curse
because Wounded Man set the bar high. Very few men I
dated after him were nearly as interesting. On the other
hand, very few were as emotionally elusive. He made me
realize that spectacular men do exist, and that I could attract them. He liked the fact that I was smart and complicated, and he made me feel oh-so-sexy, and . . . normal. In
fact, he's the guy who got me to the moment when I could
finally say, "Oh, *this* is what everyone is always going on
about."

During the early months of separation I met men almost constantly, largely through the wonders of online
dating. Every time I signed on to my Web site of choice, I
was transported to man heaven, where zillions of hunky
divorced dads dwelled. These were the forty-something
versions of guys I'd met at frat parties twenty years before
and had been too scared to deal with.

They were sandy-haired and brunet; Jersey guys and mid-

westerners; investment bankers, lawyers, and college professors. Their photos showed them hugging their children,
drinking beer on sailboats, and dressed in tuxes at formal
banquets. Many of them wrote sweetly about their desire to
share their lives with a woman. *I'm out here launching my
intentions into cyberspace because I'm ready for a partner,
and I thought I'd give serendipity a nudge,* wrote one.

There were some jerks, however, including one serial
dater who seemed always to be online, looking to score.
His dating headline read: *Total Package!* and the first few
lines of his profile read: *Not your "Average Joe," my age
and height are honest! Everything works . . . please view
my pictures for my physical appearance.*

Daily I was bombarded with charming e-mail from men
telling me I was beautiful and smart and wonderful. (True
example #1: *You are clearly an exceptionally warm, smart
and charming woman . . . and a superb mom! And, btw,
your photos are terrific.* True example #2: *Hello, you came
up in my weekly matches and immediately caught my eye.
"Wow . . . there she is, my dream girl."*) Often this flattery
got them quite far: phone calls and, sometimes, dates. I got
into a routine of going out on most Monday nights, rushing home from work to change into the middle-aged version of a sexy outfit. (Short black skirt, tights, pink tank
top, cropped sweater, high-heeled boots.) On the nights
my ex-husband had the kids, I was almost always out on
dates. The vast majority of them were simple one-date
wonders—but not all.

Among my early triumphs was a gorgeous blond. One evening I was cruising among the ads and happened upon a photo of a beautiful man. Windswept hair, chiseled features, posed next to a red Maserati. I must have him, I thought.

We e-mailed, then we talked on the phone, then he went to Italy for two weeks on business. By the time he came home, we were desperate to meet each other in person. I will confess, the moment I laid eyes on him, I thought Maserati Man seemed awfully, well, short—he was perhaps five foot eight, though I wanted to believe, in viewing his photos, that he would seem more like six feet. (My ex-husband is six four.) And there was the problem of his being uneducated and a little coarse. But he was sexy, funny, and surprisingly smart. Among the things I remember most about him was that he was taken with my skin, constantly telling me it was soft and peachy. He lasted about a month until I realized he was not a keeper—so he got the boot.

Soon after, I dated and slept with a car dealer (too boring to waste words on) and a computer geek (likewise). I was always careful, always took precautions. And in truth, it mostly wasn't about sex. (Really!) It was mostly about my personal journey, my research. Later in that first year of separation, I got an e-mail that read, in part: *I am an intelligent, decent, caring individual who appears on the surface to share many of your interests and beliefs. I have been told I am honest to a fault, and I assure you I am considered very good-looking (and modest at the same time)*. I responded, in part (note the stellar prose): *Thanks for your compliment! You sound very nice and very interesting.* Before long, I met this very good-looking guy at a diner in a neighboring town. He was amazingly handsome. I was instantly hooked, as was he.

This one would turn out to be Relationship Guy—the man from whom I learned love, longing, and infatuation for eight blissful months. If Wounded Man and I had hysterical chemistry, Relationship Guy and I had intense and deeply soulful passion. He would stare into my eyes as he made love to me, something I'd rarely experienced before. We had so much fun in bed that we would often laugh with joy. Just sleeping next to his naked body transported me.

Alas, Relationship Guy did not really want a relationship. One night he drove over to my house, threw my key at me, and proclaimed, "We're done!" I mourned his passing for a year, drinking red wine and breaking into tears while listening to bad early-seventies love songs by the Carpenters. However, I was still on my man mission. Which meant that soon after I got the ax, I went back to the dating world to lick my wounds. I still had half a dozen men to go.

Next up was Intense Guy. We had a near-instant emotional bond in writing and over the phone. He was the most emotionally mature man I've ever met—and he was precocious, too, since he was only forty-two at the time. (He boasted to me that he was unusually good with his emotions for a guy under age fifty.) He was addicted to the music of Paul Weller, was tallish, had a handsome face, and was sweet, smart, and gentle. On our first date, we went to dinner and a movie and began making out in the theater. We decided to cook together at my house for date number two. Which, of course, meant that we were going to sleep together. Which we did. Unfortunately, Intense Guy was not very intense in bed, lovely as he was in every other way.

A couple months later, I met Airplane Guy. At age fifty-one, he was the oldest of the mission men. He was among the richest I dated—all four of his kids were at boarding school, he owned a few companies, and he flew his own airplane. The money was cool, but in truth I actually liked him because he was kindhearted and gentle and had worked his way up to wealth from a blue-collar background. He possessed derring-do combined with a delicious sweetness that came from his southern upbringing.

On date number one, we went to a hip Manhattan sushi restaurant, where he ordered me the first mojito I'd ever drunk. We then proceeded to kiss and grope. Eventually, he called a limousine to take me home to the suburbs . . . a stretch limo.

The Cinderella scene lasted only through date two, when he flew his airplane to a small airport near my house for a planned overnight stay. (He lived about eighty miles away.) Boy, did I ever like telling my friends that the guy I was dating flew to see me. We made tenderloin steaks in my kitchen, ate our dinners by the fire, then went upstairs to make love. Like I said, he was sweet, but there were not a lot of sexual fireworks. The next morning, he asked me if I ever dated younger men, at which point I realized I was probably a little too energetic for him.

That experience led, a couple months later, to Younger Man. What older Airplane Guy lacked in the fireworks department, this young thing more than made up for. He was not especially handsome or tall, but he was mighty energetic and sexy. I loved the fact that he could program my iPod and introduce me to music sung by people significantly younger than me. I loved that he found me irresistible even though I was eight years older. I loved meeting him after work at bars frequented by thirty-somethings. And I loved his carefree lifestyle.

Unfortunately, by about the third month, I began to find him annoying—he was flat-out obnoxious, and his carefree lifestyle started to seem pathetic. When he announced he was leaving for Peru, I was delighted. When he came back three weeks later I saw him a couple more times, until he left again—this time for India. He wrote me a few e-mails from Asia, but at that point I decided the ego rush of dating a younger guy wasn't worth the irritation.

There were a few more encounters with the hothothot Wounded Man around this time, then a three-month stint with man number eleven—CPA Guy. He was quite funny (once describing a springtime ant infestation in his condo as "the insurgents of Fallujah"), and he was definitely a great suburban father—my kinda guy. He was easy, uncomplicated, and a good kisser. But for some reason, we couldn't get up the passion mojo, and I began to view going on dates with him as an opportunity to have sex like a man. In other words, "Why not?" Finally, he had the guts to call a spade a spade, and he put us both out of our misery on tax day—a couple hours after he'd mailed in the last of the returns he'd been working on during our entire relationship.

And that gets us to today, a moment when I have reached some sort of serenity about it all, after nearly three years of dating. I'm not on a mission anymore, though I do occasionally go on dates. I've reached my modest numerical goal and now feel confident that I'm sexually experienced enough to hold my own in any sex conversation or any bedroom romp. There will, unfortunately, be a few more conquests on the way to finding My Guy—but I don't plan on too many more.

The other night I was home alone on a Saturday night, relieved to have solitude. One of my neighbors, a gay man in a committed relationship, came over to talk. We got chatting about dating, and he told me that when he was single, he would cruise the online ads, ultimately going on some two hundred coffee dates. Never, he said, did he meet anyone he was interested in having a relationship with. And only a couple times did he meet someone he slept with.

Then one day at a party, he looked across the room and saw the man who would become his partner, and with whom he would adopt three children, buy a house, and raise a family. "The universe spoke to me," he said.

I thought about that the whole following week—even while I was still checking into the online dating world. But since I don't have a goal anymore, I'm not sure there's a point to writing, flirting, talking, meeting, eating, drinking, dating—and then taking my clothes off.

Except there is that cute guy in man heaven, a nice forty-something dad in the 'burbs . . . that guy who wrote, "I thought I'd give serendipity a nudge."

Okay, maybe one more.

MECHANICAL FAILURE
by Stephan Wilkinson

It's an urban legend that the Inuits have 400 words for snow, but it's absolutely true that the online encyclopedia *Wikipedia* lists 650 synonyms in English alone (okay, 648 in English and 2 in Yiddish) for a single small piece of male anatomy. Call it dick, prick or willy, johnson or peter, schlong, schwantz, stiffy, pecker, dong, unit, package, dork, one-eyed snake, trouser hose, beaver cleaver, wang, woody, or wiener, it's all the same thing. A penis. Like so many things sexual, the male reproductive tool has far more euphemisms than it needs, perhaps because people talk about those forbidden things so much that they get tired of using the same old word.

Actually, I didn't really talk—or certainly write—all that much about my own penis until I no longer had one.

It isn't entirely accurate, that assertion about my penis, but it's close. I still have one, but it's a shadow of its former self, a puppy dick peeking shyly out of a tangled bush, and it no longer works.

I had a prostatectomy at sixty, the all-too-common operation performed to excise prostate cancer. In the majority of cases, particularly among men in their late fifties or older, the procedure also snips the nerve that provokes an erection. No erection, no sex. At least, no standard, conventional, in-and-out sex.

Maybe I should have had radiation treatment, or chemotherapy, or the newly popular seed implantation, a form of precision nuclear zapping that involves the minimally invasive injection of tiny radioactive capsules into the cancerous prostate, though all of those procedures carry the risk of impotence as well. No sense what-iffing, though, because I didn't. My wife and I—and it best be a mutual decision—opted for full-frontal surgery.

I frankly don't do anything without my wife's approval, in large part because she's so much smarter and more mature than I am despite being sixteen years younger. We'd been married for eighteen years when I had my prostatectomy, and sex had ranged from a frantic twice a day to a placid twice a month. Not because Susan isn't just as physically appealing as she was when we met—she a long-legged, miniskirted, job-hunting Middlebury grad and me a once-divorced magazine editor who persuaded my boss to hire her—but because even though she spent more than twenty hours a week at the gym and had the body of a twenty-five-year-old athlete, in a sense we were having too much fun doing lots of other things to bother with a lot of sex.

I wasn't surprised that Susan favored surgery. She's decisive and a rationalist. And I suspect she talked it over with our daughter, then seventeen. (Brook grew up learning that families do not have secrets.)

My wife has a friend whose husband was recently about to undergo a prostatectomy, and Susan confided to her that I'd been impotent since my surgery. "I don't care about that happening," her friend said. "Maybe I would if I were twenty, but right now, I just want that damn tumor gone." After the operation, her husband turned out to be one of the lucky ones who retained "erectile function," as the polite phrase has it. "Tell you the truth, I was secretly hoping that he wouldn't," Susan's friend later admitted. "It's been a long marriage . . ."

Okay, some things men would rather not know.

One thing they don't bother to tell you before prostate surgery is that even if you can still get erections, a prostatectomy will shorten your dick. No, they don't cut the head off, but the effect is the same.

The prostate gland is usually described as being about the size of a walnut—let's say an inch in diameter, though I've seen them twice as big in medical exhibits—and it surrounds the urethra, which is the tube leading to and through the penis, through which passes urine as well as the ejaculate that is produced by the prostate. Cut the prostate out and, like slicing a leaky piece out of an old garden hose, you're also eliminating an inch or two of the urethra. Now the doc has to reattach the two severed ends of the tube, and he takes the slack with which to do it not from your internals, where there's no give, but from the external penis, essentially pulling it that much closer to your belly. Like shorter.

It didn't really bother me afterward, at least not the way I'm sure the disfigurement of a radical mastectomy would traumatize a woman. After all, my dick didn't work anymore in any case, and certainly Susan was cool enough not to mention it.

After my operation, I went to a highly regarded sexologist/urologist for possible help, the kind of guy who's in every talk-show address book for when they need a dick doc to talk about the latest ED pill. (Viagra and the like, incidentally, are useless for people like me. If the nerve that phones ahead the erection request is missing, there's not much that pharmacology can do. Well, except for one interesting semicure that I'll get to.) The sexpert didn't actually laugh when he saw my penis, but he did say, "Hmmm, that's some substantial atrophy." Thanks, Doc.

Here's how we manipulated my poor little peter after Viagra proved powerless:

First I tried the pump, which has to be one of the most hilarious devices this side of the Arawak penis sheath. The Pump is a transparent plastic can that you put over your limp dick, holding it as airtightly as possible against your hairy abdomen while hysterically wobbling a handle much like one of those things that evacuates the air to save a half-empty bottle of wine. Somehow, the substantially reduced atmospheric pressure this creates inside the plastic can draws a trickle of extra blood into the spongy core of the penis, and the result is a semierection.

As you pop the can off your sort-of stiffy, you then have to quickly slide a tight rubber band down to the base of the penis to keep the extra blood from draining back out. If everything goes reasonably well, you hobble from the bathroom back into the bedroom, bent over from the pain and embarrassment, and achieve penetration. (The pressure needed to part the typical National Bureau of Standards vagina is three and a half pounds. I suppose you could make a small weight and balance it atop your artificial erection. If the flesh is stiffly willing, you're good to go. If it crumples, more pumping is called for.)

Though the Pump worked, it was rather like having intercourse with a manufactured penis, and it put me in mind of a friend's remark when we were gossiping about a physically unattractive woman we both knew. "I wouldn't fuck her with your dick," my friend said. I ultimately decided I wouldn't fuck my wife with the Pump's dick and turned to the next choice: injections.

Many people have a needle phobia, and the thought of poking a hollow, stainless steel syringe into their lap rocket curls their toes, straightens their hair, and makes their teeth itch. But needlesticks don't bother me a bit, so Susan and I moved to the next level, which was for her to gently inject 10cc of something called Caverject through a hair-thin needle of the kind used by diabetics to give themselves daily insulin injections straight into the corpus cavernosum to chemically excite an erection.

It worked, and it hurt about as much as a mosquito bite, but it also put me in mind of yet another friend to whom I'd gone for advice because I'd been told that he too had a can't-get-it-up problem. His dysfunction was emotional, not surgical, but he also had tried the injection solution. "Oh, jeez," Jerry said, "you mix up the cocktail of meds, you get the needle ready, you fill the syringe and do the whole thing, and then, fine, you fuck your wife. If Sharon Stone came through the bedroom door, I'd do it again in a heartbeat, but otherwise, it's a waste of time."

I had run out of answers. Actually, there was one left, but neither Susan nor I wanted to consider it: a penile implant. This is in fact an ancient solution, and the original implants were a transplanted piece of rib that literally gave you a permanently stiff penis. Modern implants can be similarly stiff-but-bendable artificial boners, so they can be tucked away between bedroom bouts. But the gold standard for transplantable objects is the inflatable, flexible bladder, like a skinny hot dog, that takes up residence inside the penis, alongside the urethra. It's pumped up, *foof-foof-foof-foof,* by a little bulb that is put into—where else?—the otherwise-useless scrotum.

We imagined the foreplay opportunities—"No, honey, that's the pump, not a testicle"—but decided the risk of that much surgical intervention wasn't worth the Roman candle. (The operation typically costs more than twenty thousand dollars, and if complications arise, which can occur from shifting of the implant, the expense of repairing the device can be even greater.)

Because I'm open about my impotence, friends have quietly come to me and asked for prostatectomy advice, which of course I'm happy to provide, for what it's worth. Perhaps the strangest such contact I had was with an acquaintance who told me his father had been biopsied and found to have early-stage prostate cancer. He didn't want to even discuss surgery or any other treatment, though. Didn't care if he died, or how painful it might be, because he couldn't imagine not being able to ejaculate.

I'm hardly alone in possessing minimal equipment. Despite all the evidence to the contrary, there's hardly a man alive who doesn't secretly—or openly—believe that bigger is better, though few actually are well endowed.

Evidence to the contrary? Well, Michelangelo's *David* has probably the most famous and certainly most visible dick in the world, and scaled down to life-size, it probably goes a good three and a half flaccid inches. Michelangelo supposedly was gay, in which case you wouldn't think he'd be particularly reticent about sculpting a grand wiener.

In fact, no legitimate artwork that I can think of, with the exception of Robert Mapplethorpe's photography, shows a schlong anything like what men imagine every other guy is packing. Hercules, Adam, David, Leonardo da Vinci's famous proportionate *Vitruvian Man* . . . all are classically depicted with penes that make it apparent why codpieces—initially simply a jockstrap-like piece of clothing—were embellished to exaggerate the size of the wearer's unit: There wasn't much there in the first place.

There's the occasional exception to the size-matters rule. I recently read in *The Week* magazine that Latin singer Enrique Iglesias, the boyfriend of tennis hottie Anna Kournikova, is considering endorsing a line of extra-small condoms for men as slightly hung as he says he is. "I can never find extra-small condoms, and I know from experience that it's really embarrassing," he said. Embarrassing to not find them or embarrassing to have to ask for them?

Lord knows I daren't do more than hint at the possibility that athlete/novelist/movie-star-handsome manly man John Irving is minimally hung, since he was a nationally ranked collegiate wrestler not that long ago and could kick my skinny ass. But his spectacular novel *Until I Find You* is a presumptively drawn-from-life, personal, 800-page evocation of the adventures of a small-dicked boy-man who eventually has inventive sex with every woman who comes within a block of him.

Fact is, the average erect penis is only five and a half inches long, and even that number is suspect, since men with larger schlongs are more likely to participate in measurement studies than are Thumbelinas. ("Do you know why women can't estimate measurements?" my brother Leland once said, in the only dirty joke that holder of a Harvard Divinity School degree has ever told me. "Because all their lives, they've been told *this* is ten inches," he said, holding a thumb and forefinger five inches apart.)

I've never been a locker-room peeker, never given much thought to the natural endowment of other men, but it certainly seems to be a matter of fascination to many guys. Okay, I'm an Internet peeker: There's a Web site, www.imagesofsize.com, that offers three thousand close-up photos of penes—which, pronounced "peenies," is a plural of penis, if you want to win a bar bet—of every size, shape, acute angle, and race. The angular dangle is called Peyronie's disease, a term we learned when Monica Lewinsky announced that the First Dick had a distinctive shape. But what is particularly interesting about the site is the number of pictures of men with the tiniest peepees you can imagine. I'm talking an inch . . . half an inch . . . an inch erect, even. It's reassuring to many of us to see that others have the same or even less to work with than we do.

Talk to women who are willing to be honest about what works for them, and you'll find that if anything, circumference is more pleasurable than length. Having one's cervix slammed isn't particularly desirable, apparently. What matters infinitely more than length, girth, or circumference is, in fact, distance. The long-distance runners are definitely not lonely when it comes to sex.

Watch a good porn-film performer bring to multiple orgasms a woman he's just met that morning and whose name he doesn't remember, and you know that size is not what impresses. And not just for women. As far as porn producers are concerned, the real moneymakers are actors who not only can produce serial ejaculations but also can come on command. *I had a guy with a five-inch erection,* one porn-film producer recently posted on an Internet sex-film bulletin board, *and I used him constantly, if only as a stand-in for the money shot. He saved me thousands of dollars a day of shooting. I could do two films in the time it normally took to do one. If you can come over and over and do it exactly when I say so, your porn career is assured.*

My porn career never even got started, but if it had, perhaps I'd have resorted to the marketers of various mechanical devices intended to increase penis size. They often refer to the penis as a muscle that needs to be exercised in order to get bigger and stronger. If that were true, men who masturbated constantly would be the best-hung of all. The penis, of course, is no more a muscle than is the brain. The heart is a muscle. Pecs and abs are muscles. The penis is a simple machine, a tubular sponge that uses hydraulic fluid—blood—to enable its work. The only muscles involved are those in the lower back that do the manly thrusting.

Still, lots of men want to lengthen their penes, and marketers have come up with an array of ways to give the appearance of doing so, though in fact you can no more increase penis size than you can build brainpower or improve your eyesight. There are pumps, there are regimens that involve walking around with weights hung from the member—presumably involving front-pleated, wide-legged pants—and there are manipulations you can do that involve jerking your poor johnson in and out and from side to side hard enough to "break down the internal cellular structure so that it regrows larger and longer."

Wow. Thank goodness that's something I no longer have to consider as an option.

Of course, there are lots of more pleasant things I can no longer consider as options either. Yes, such as intercourse. But into its third decade, our marriage has—like Susan's gym friend's—been a long one. We've moved far beyond the time when the conjunction of soft and hard flesh, friction in the dark, and exchanging bodily fluids often seemed to be the point of it all. Besides, there are other ways to make love. And look on the good side: Now nobody has to sleep on the wet spot.

So for me, ultimately, the pee in penis has become the organ's sole meaning. My little dork has become an exceedingly simple tool, no longer a machine, through which I urinate. Works for me.

What's Sex Got to Do with It?

by Susan Crandell

⌒ The other day, the *Today* show did a segment about what women really want from their love life, featuring a survey in which 47 percent of women ranked cuddling as more important, versus a mere 25 percent who'd rather have sex. This is hardly breaking news to the nation's women. Women's magazines have long published statistics pointing out that physical closeness is more cherished than the actual act. But for the majority of guys, the bedroom is a sporting arena, a venue of victory or defeat. You won't see hugs-versus-sex scores reported on ESPN. When it comes to sexual agendas, we're like conservatives who only watch the news on Fox or liberals whose radio is perma-tuned to NPR. Women have the reputation of not caring much about sex, but nobody asks the follow-up question: What is it that we do want?

I know what I want: a husband who stays alive.

Steve and I faced the question of how central intercourse is to our marriage when he had a prostatectomy that left him impotent when he was sixty and I was forty-five. From the moment we heard the biopsy report, I had one thought in mind: Please, just let me keep this guy. When his surgeon explained the less-than-appealing potential outcomes of surgery—incontinence, impotence—it didn't slow me down a bit. Damn the side effects, full speed ahead. I wanted that cancer out of his body and in a jar. So did Steve, and there was no argument that this was the course of treatment he should take.

After all, we were embarking on our third decade of sex together. Who could be so greedy as to ask for more than that? When Steve and I married, in the late seventies, I felt invincible. We were young, we were healthy, sex was great, and within a year we had a baby. There's a little bronze sign under a shade tree in our backyard: BENEATH THIS TREE WERE WED STEPHAN WILKINSON AND SUSAN CRANDELL. A FRUITFUL BOND SOON TO FLOWER AND EVER TO ENDURE. When we added Brook's name to the plaque, our life was perfect, complete. The frequency of sex may have waned over the years, but if quantity was down, quality was still AAA. Until that day in his doctor's office, I thought sex was something we'd always have.

Maybe that's because I'm a boomer. Remember the

summer of love? We claim we invented recreational sex, though it may actually be simply a matter of timing: We were lucky enough to come of age sexually in that golden moment post-pill and pre-AIDS, when bad sex meant you didn't climax, not that you died. Surely, we thought, someday we'll be shaking the walls of the old-age home.

When prostate surgery put the brakes on our sex life, I was so thankful the cancer hadn't spread that I couldn't think about anything else. Hmmmm, let's see: Sex life or life, sex life or life? Is that even a choice? And yet, that old Venus/Mars thing did crop up. While I looked forward to many years of emotional intimacy, Steve despaired that we might never have sex again.

Nobody can say we didn't give alternative methods a try. I may have had my eye on the real prize—Steve's continued good health—but neither of us was going to let our sex life go down without a fight. Steve received a prescription for Viagra the very day it came on the market—no joy— and he labored manfully with a medieval torture device to pump up his penis. I remember lying in bed one night, candles burning, music playing, listening to him smash the pump onto the bathroom floor in frustration (luckily the pump was sturdy stuff; we were still able to return it for a full refund at the end of the thirty-day trial period).

Turns out, when Viagra doesn't work, Pfizer can up-grade you: They've got another little erectile re-function system called Caverject Impulse Therapy. Yes, that's *ject* as in *inject*, and it is Little Stevie who's going to get shot.

How important is intercourse? Important enough to Steve and me to report to his urologist for a lesson on proper Caverject technique. The doctor, a talkative midforties guy with a Hindi lilt and a passion for drawing diagrams, sketches out a penis with its chambers, or corpora cavernosa, that fill with blood to create an erection. Shoot that Caverject juice in there, and in no time Little Stevie will be standing at attention.

Ajit, the urologist, demonstrates how to do the deed, injecting Steve and all the while chattering away about how when I perform the injection at home, I must be careful not to nick an artery or punch a hole in the urethra. Now here's the really fun part: Like Viagra, the Caverject doesn't work on its own; you've got to create the mood. Exiting the examination room, the doctor tells us to get busy so he can see whether this is going to be the answer for us. The walls are so thin I can hear somebody whispering a couple of rooms down. After two decades of marriage, sex is suddenly awkward again. I mean, are we talking hand job here, or am I supposed to drop my pants and climb up on the examining table? And what about poor Steve—how is he possibly going to get in the mood? Suddenly I have oceans of empathy for all the guys who've stood in stalls at doctors' offices wretchedly paging through old, dog-eared issues of *Hustler* to provide a sperm sample. In deference to my mother, whom I fervently hope never reads this, I will withhold the details. Suffice to say, we have liftoff. Ajit returns to admire Steve's erection, and we're in business.

We now have an erectile system that will work—that is, if I am willing to stick a needle in my husband's dick every time we want to make love. Steve, who doesn't give blood because it involves such a big needle, is gung ho. I chalk this up as one more example of men's one-track minds—intercourse at any cost. Medical school is an unrealized dream of mine, so while I can't say I'm eager to jab a needle into the man I love, I'm not squeamish about it either.

Our druggist outfits us with a box of hypodermics (Steve later rinses out the empties and uses them for some arcane ritual involving the model airplanes he builds) and two little vials of the Caverject elixir (I note that this stuff is unpopular enough to require a special order). Tonight's the night.

I am not going to be cruel enough to ask gentlemen readers to put themselves in Steve's place, but for you women, I'd like to pause a moment here so you can imagine sticking your husband in the penis with a hypodermic. To think that we used to say inserting a diaphragm was a mood killer. This is the big league.

It isn't what I'd call a normal sex life. Here's the drill. We head to the bedroom, get all cozy. When the moment is right, I pad downstairs to the refrigerator and fetch the little vial of magic fluid (of course I've forgotten to pick up the supplies before we got going and now have to assemble everything on the bedside table: hypodermic, check; sterile gauze wipe, check; stiffy fluid, check) and wash my hands like I'm scrubbing up for surgery. I fill the hypodermic, then tap the side and give it a jaunty little squirt to make sure all the air is out. I locate the right spot (now that I think of it, a tattoo would be mighty useful), stick the needle in, and confirm the positioning by drawing a little blood into the syringe. Finally, I push the plunger. Once I remove the needle and press an alcohol wipe to the spot until the bleeding stops, we're good to go.

We do it, it works, and afterward we sit in bed grinning goofily. Next morning, Steve calls Ajit to see how often we're allowed to do this. Twice a week? Twice a day? Twice an hour?

You can tell that we are seriously sex-starved because a week later, we're back in the doctor's office raving about the Caverject. We are having regular sex. It's a miracle. Why doesn't everybody do this? He tells us few are willing to even try it, and almost everybody quits after a couple of months. "That Ajit—what a spoilsport," we tell each other as we drive home, shaking our heads at the folly of people who would forfeit a chance at good old-fashioned sex.

We continue to have hypodermic-enhanced intercourse for nearly a year, but eventually we too become Caverject dropouts, just as Ajit had predicted. I never got totally comfortable with jamming a needle into Steve's penis. The fact that my aim wasn't faultless and sometimes the injection failed didn't help. In the end, it was like the MasterCard ad: knowing that we could have sex was priceless. But the cost of actually doing it—the mood killing, the dick pricking, the uncertainty of success—was too high. Finally, we figured out that plenty of fun could be had without my Nurse Diesel impersonation.

Along the way, we discovered the real meaning of intimacy: that sex pales in the face of love. The best part of going to a party is lying in bed together afterward, gossiping. Steve installed a home theater in our bedroom, and the marital bed is now a comfy place to watch movies on the eight-foot screen that pulls down over the closet doors. We lounge against big piles of pillows, dipping into a bottomless bowl of popcorn. We can talk if we want to, or even throw popcorn at the screen. Yes, we are that pathetic couple who sit at dinner and talk about their cat. We can't get it up to fight the way we used to. The old arguments, like why he deposits drain hair on the bathtub edge, or why I leave the kitchen countertop speckled with water in the exact spot where he always sets the newspaper down, just don't seem that important anymore. It's amazing that they ever did. As for sex, we do what we can and don't worry about what we can't. By the time you're fifty you've figured out that life's too short for regrets.

Two years ago, I quit my staff editor's job to freelance write. Now Steve and I both work from home, and friends ask me, "How can you stand it? Don't you drive each other crazy?" Not at all. I'm just so grateful to have the love of my life here for the long haul, not to mention all that extra time to cuddle.

Part III

ALL THE WISER

WRINKLES IN TIME
by Joyce Maynard

I remember the first time I heard about Botox. This was probably five years ago, which would have put me somewhere in the second half of my forties. Poking fifty with a short stick, as a former sweetheart of mine would have put it—though when he introduced me to that concept, the milestone I was approaching was forty. At the time, I supposed that meant I was old.

Now another milestone loomed ominously. I was old enough, at this point, to understand plenty about the aging process, and all the ways—subtle and not so subtle—in which the passage of years transforms whatever we have come to know as our face and our body. Not an easy business, this one.

You think you know what you look like in the mirror,

and then, slowly, the reflection changes. First it's microscopic: a single gray hair, the shadow of a line around the mouth, or not even a line, only the suggestion of the place where the line will one day reside.

By my midforties, I had grown accustomed to the idea that every four weeks or so (six, if I was feeling lazy) I'd spend an evening coloring my hair. Where for the first thirty-five years of my life I had taken my skin for granted, somewhere around the four-decade mark, I'd recognized the need to wear sunscreen and apply moisturizer.

My weight hadn't fluctuated more than a pound or two from what was printed on the driver's license I'd been issued in my late thirties, but it sat on me differently now, as I recognized in the locker room of my gym, passing the naked bodies of the women fifteen years younger than me (and those of the women fifteen years older—a disheartening warning of what lay ahead, even, apparently, for those of us who got to a gym on a regular basis). Then came a new and alarming discovery: while in the past I had taken a certain pride in my legs, I caught a glimpse of them in a mirror one day and saw, to my horror, that my knees looked like someone else's now—as if a bunch of fabric in need of ironing had come off the curtains and gathered up around at the midleg point— and the knees I'd known as mine had gone away.

All of this I knew, and if I hadn't exactly come to terms with it all—the gray hair, the lines around the mouth, a less well rounded rear end, and wrinkled knees—I had at least become familiar with these aspects of the landscape I inhabited now, as a woman who had, without question, entered middle age. Still, when I read in a magazine about this amazing new procedure gaining in popularity, in which supposedly sane women all around the major metropolitan areas of America were ponying up a few hundred dollars to have a drug injected into their foreheads for the purpose of temporarily paralyzing their frown lines (and thereby smoothing out the creases for a few months), I shook my head with amazement. In fact, I read, Botox was actually a form of poison. And women were lining up to get shot up with it.

"What crazy idea will our youth-obsessed culture think up next," I said to my friend T, "for women to abuse their bodies in the name of vanity and try to deny the aging process?"

My friend on the other end of the telephone was silent for an unusually long time. Then she spoke, but in a quiet voice, oddly subdued for her.

"Actually, Joyce," she told me, "I just had a Botox injection myself last week. The results were amazing."

She was the first of a rapidly growing list of female friends and acquaintances in my circle—serious, intelligent women who had careers and belonged to NARAL and attended book discussion groups—who started heading off to the dermatologist around that time to get their shot of poison in the forehead. And so, as the months passed, I found my eyes turning more and more to the brows of the women I knew, around my age, and I discovered that a surprising number of them now seemed startlingly free of the lines I myself had there. Lines whose depth, like that of some rapidly eroding canyon, seemed to grow on a daily basis.

It's an insidious thing, what happens when you let an idea creep into your brain, first as an idle fantasy, perhaps. Initially, all I did was ask my friends how much this procedure cost. The answer: $250 per visit, usually. At least, that would buy you an injection into the location of the two parallel lines that sat like parentheses between the eyebrows—a pair of lines I'd first observed around age thirty-five, that I hated not only because they made me look older but also because, according to my children, they made me look mad all the time.

If you wanted to iron out not only those two lines but also the tracks above them, you were looking at a second injection. Another two hundred bucks, most likely. And of course that only covered you for a few months, till the paralysis wore off, at which point a return visit—and another check—would be required.

Still, as the months passed, it seemed more and more as if wherever I went, the women I knew were looking younger, more carefree. Frown lines gone. Foreheads as smooth as a baby's bottom.

My seemingly idle inquiries into cost led to step two, of course. One night, applying the expensive moisturizer I now invested in (rather than the old standby of my thirties,

Noxzema) I stretched the skin of my forehead taut, just to get an idea of what I'd look like without those lines.

I looked better. Not only younger, but happier. Within twenty-four hours, I had an appointment at a place called Simple Radiance for my first injection. That was four years ago.

Now for a brief lesson in Botox. The first time I got an injection, although the difference in my forehead was dramatic, it wore off in under three months, and when the paralysis subsided, the lines returned. But as I continued to undergo the procedure, its effects not only disguised existing lines but—most miraculously—removed them, in much the same way that placing a piece of canvas on a stretcher for a period of months or placing one's pants over a pants dryer actually eliminates whatever creases might have been there before. So pretty soon, instead of returning to Simple Radiance every twelve weeks, I could let sixteen weeks pass, even eighteen, without returning to the old, mad-looking forehead.

I didn't go out of my way to announce this, but I made a decision early on about this new ritual of mine: I wouldn't lie about it. When a woman friend raised the topic of Botox—and it was striking how often the topic came up—I volunteered that I myself partook of the procedure. Vanity and overinvestment in the appearance of youth might well be among my failings, but I wasn't about to add deceitfulness or shame to the list. And really, I decided, what was so terrible about indulging in a harmless, noninvasive cosmetic procedure a few times a year. I didn't gamble, didn't smoke, didn't drink hard liquor, drive a gas-guzzling vehicle, or buy furs. Who was I hurting with a little poison injected into the muscles over my brow now and then?

The response of my friends to all of this varied considerably. For a few, the fact that I admitted to getting Botox injections evidently provided the affirmation they had needed to do it themselves. Others were horrified. We were that generation, after all, who'd come of age during the great years of revived feminist activism, when *Ms.* magazine had come into being, along with the *Roe v. Wade* Supreme Court decision, and the campaign for passage of the Equal Rights Amendment. We were the first to be admitted to previously all-male colleges, and then we'd gone on, many of us, to law school and med school and Wall Street. (Less often, to the maternity ward. I had been rare, among my friends, in choosing to have my first child at twenty-four and two more after that before the age of thirty-one.)

But as much as we'd been shaped by feminism, our positions had taken on a certain element of realism, too, with age. It was one thing to say at twenty-two or twenty-eight (with our bellies firm and our faces unlined) that for too long, women's looks had been far too much of a factor in their lives and should be irrelevant. Easy enough to say, when you are young and slim and pretty, that you want to be recognized only for your talents and skills, your hard work and accomplishment.

At fifty, those same women who once railed at the uninvited attentions of men (in the workplace, or walking past a construction site) may find, to their amazement, that they miss them. Once, we complained that men didn't take us seriously enough. We were just sex objects. Then we weren't sex objects anymore, and instead of being taken more seriously, what many of us felt was the loss of a kind of power we had too long taken for granted.

"Some time along the line, in the last ten years or so," a friend of mine said, in a quiet voice filled with sadness, "I realized I'd become invisible."

It's not that my chief stock-in-trade was ever my looks. I wasn't a beauty—wasn't a model or a movie star or a ballerina or any of those professions in which the attainment of a certain age means, for a woman, almost certain retirement. The kind of work I do carries no age limit, and the things for which I've been most appreciated have nothing to do with the smoothness of my forehead, the brown of my hair.

And still, I found, as fifty approached (and then, after I passed it) that I wasn't ready to throw in the towel altogether where my physical attractiveness was concerned. I liked dressing up and putting on makeup and flirting, for fun, at parties, with the confidence that comes of knowing one still looks at least reasonably good, as opposed to (here comes another phrase once uttered by a sweetheart of mine) "mutton posing as lamb." I liked feeling pretty, if not on a daily basis, at least now and then.

But the losses that come with diminished ability to

attract male attention go beyond those suffered by the ego. Because for a woman with a career, whether she's an anchorperson or an engineer, there are few places where her looks won't feature as some kind of a factor in how she's perceived in her profession. Whether or not it was politically correct to undergo artificial procedures to banish lines, the fact is that as long as I live in a society where lines signify a certain diminishment of power for a woman, I prefer not to have them.

A person might well ask—and I have—what kind of power it really is that a woman possesses, if all it's about is looking young and pretty, being slim and free from lines on her face, with hair untouched by silver. What we lose as we age is nothing more than the power to seduce, perhaps. And if the only way we can manage to get someplace in life is through our attractiveness and desirability, is that even a place we should care about getting to?

A person might also point out—and I do—all the wonderful-looking women who continue to look not only attractive but deeply desirable into their sixties and beyond, not with the assistance of age-concealing procedures but through their own natural and ageless beauty. Look at the gorgeously voluptuous figure of Sophia Loren, I tell myself. Look at Emmylou Harris with her silver hair. And I can name other women too—not entertainers, but writers and thinkers, teachers and grandmothers (my own mother among them), who have not lost the ability to turn heads when they walk into a room.

Intelligence and character and experience and humor shine from within these women, regardless of the lines on their faces. These women may have lost their smooth foreheads, or their girlish figures, or their golden hair. But they have managed to preserve the ability of being viewed as attractive women. Maybe they did this without Botox, but if you ask me, no woman should feel guilty or ashamed for doing what she can to hold on to that part of life, by whatever means, and for whatever time she is able to.

Here is the dirty little secret most women over forty-five will tell you, if they're honest. However smart we are, or talented, or funny, or good, it is an inescapable aspect of being female that we will also be viewed—and ultimately assessed—in terms of how we look.

You can buy into it, as I do when I perform my hundred sit-ups every morning and, with a certain amount of regret, let the bread basket pass me by at dinner. And as I do when I let the dermatologist press an ice pack against my forehead quarterly to numb the place where the Botox needle goes in.

Or you can throw your hands in the air, throw your brassieres in the trash, reach for the chocolates, and say, "Let the world go to hell. I don't care what anybody thinks but me anymore." Either way, either choice, carries with it a set of restrictions on our lives. For the woman who puts out so much energy staving off what are known as "the ravages of time," it's the stress, work, energy, and probably money required to fight the battle; for the woman who chooses not to get into the game, it's the realization that she will be written off (though presumably only by people whose acceptance she doesn't want anymore anyway).

I understand both choices. I make mine with an awareness of its cost. Looking good at fifty-two—good for a fifty-two-year-old, anyway—is time consuming. And expensive.

It's a few months before my fifty-third birthday, and I have gone out to a bookstore near my home in California to hear a friend read from her new book. A highly intelligent and thoughtful person—well read, well traveled, a serious thinker, and a wonderful writer—my friend greets me afterward with a warm embrace. We haven't seen each other in many months. First words out of her mouth: "You're holding up well." And, truthfully, the first thought in my head when I saw her was that she looked older than I remembered.

There you have it. That's where my brain went. Same place hers did. Not to the books we've written, or read, since we last met, or to loved ones, or travels, or the news of the world, or the struggles within, but to how well each of us is "holding up."

Sometimes I wonder what it would feel like not to care about this stuff. I think about all the extra time I'd have if I didn't spend one afternoon and $120 every six weeks getting my hair professionally colored now. All the concentration that currently goes into meditations on what outfit to wear, or whether to cut bangs, or whether Pilates might accomplish what the sit-ups have not (namely, flatten my stomach, which still sticks out, no matter what I do).

But lined as my face may be, I think my brain has some aging to do before I reach the place of not caring, the place of accepting, the place in which, if I'm lucky and strong enough, maybe, what I will have lost in physical appeal will be more than sufficiently compensated by character and wisdom. I may not be young enough to have a smooth forehead without benefit of Botox, but I am not yet old enough, evidently, not to care about wrinkles.

I like to think, though, that what I am doing here is not so much denying the aging process as it is weaning myself gradually, and gently, of the face and body I knew when I was young and the kind of response all women receive, to some degree, simply by virtue of being a certain age. I think I am slowly getting used to the idea of losing these things, because losing them is inevitable. I just need a little more time.

The other day, for instance, I found myself back at my dermatologist's office for my once-every-four-months shot of muscle-paralyzing poison to the forehead. Having noticed a number of new lines around my mouth, I thought I'd ask Michelle, my Botox technician, if she had any ideas for me about what to do about this. Foolishly, perhaps, I had supposed she might suggest some great new cream or lotion I could buy, and even if it cost more than what I was using at the moment, I was prepared to buy this product if it existed.

But instead, what Michelle began talking about was surgery. She was moving her hands over my face now, pointing out all the places we could take care of if I moved up to the next step: this place around the eyes where my brows might be lifted a little, a tightening around the mouth. I was doing surprisingly well with my neck, she told me, but once I was under anesthesia anyway, it might be a good idea to take a few quick tucks there too. She knew a place in Costa Rica where a bunch of her clients had gone for a fraction of the price you'd pay in the city.

And then, of course, we might take care of that place on my belly that never goes away, no matter how many sit-ups I do, how much bread I don't eat. The fold of skin three pregnancies gave me. That reminds me, every time I rest my hand on that place, of my children.

Michelle's suggestions might have signaled the beginning of a new phase in my life—the moment I crossed over the line from the needle to the knife. The images of my skin stretched tighter that were reflected back to me in the mirror might have had the same effect that once, four years ago, the image of my crease-free forehead had. The door had been opened. I could have slipped through it easily enough, and before you knew it, I might have been booking myself a ticket to Costa Rica.

Only I didn't. To my relief, I saw, I didn't want to go there. The Botox was enough—a small gift I give myself that I sometimes think of as the little reward I get for the things I do on my own, without chemical or medical assistance, to look my best. But in the end, though I won't pretend I've never thought about cosmetic surgery—and seldom meet an American woman my age who hasn't at least imagined it—I think I'll leave things where they stand: not quite ready to let age have its way with me unimpeded. But not ready to deny nature or the calendar entirely either.

For the eight thousand dollars I would pay for this surgery, I could take three of my children on a wonderful trip—someplace where there would be rain forests and volcanoes, quetzal birds, or grass huts on the beach, maybe, and wonderful exotic foods we'd never tasted. They will love me no less for the lines around my mouth, and love me no less, either, for the lines not yet on my forehead.

So there you have it—the place where I get on the train, and the place I get off. Botox, yes. Cosmetic surgery, no. (Not for now anyway. I make no ultimate predictions of the future anymore. That's one thing a half century of living has taught me.) I'm not about to judge anyone else for making a different decision. But as for me, I plan to age as gracefully as I can, which is to say not without a little quiet kicking and screaming, but slowly, very slowly, growing not just older, but wiser too.

THE GOOD-ENOUGH AFFAIR
by Alice Elliott Dark

You notice him; who wouldn't? He is very Robert Downey Jr., handsomer than normal people usually are. He walks into your writing class in an aura of purpose, his sleeves rolled up over viny forearms, his cowboy boots stamping the tiles, his errant bangs inviting a hand to push them back. Every week he takes careful notes on what you say, and when he speaks his brow crumples, as if his thoughts are so ponderous that they cause him pain. This makes you smile. If you were younger, you'd want to save him from his tortured self, but you've been there, done that, too many times not to know better. Sensibly, you gave up the adorable vampires so you could have a life and married instead someone who knows how to be nice and to think about you. This guy is not your type, not anymore.

Even if he were, RD wears a wedding ring too, and he's significantly younger than you, in his very early thirties. You recently turned forty-one. Your days of being a girl, a lover, are over. You're mostly invisible on the streets, so much so that when you bump into young guys they startle, as if they'd been touched by the cold hand of a ghost.

There's no way RD would think of you as anything other than a writing teacher, which is as it should be. You are a professional, after all. You know from transference; propriety is your byword. After the first flush of appreciation, you honestly don't give him another thought that isn't appropriate. When he walks out of the final class of the term, after a gentlemanly thank-you and a handshake, you assume you'll never see him again. Oh well. Middle age is one big map of roads not taken, past and present. Ten years earlier, RD might have been your highway to heaven. At least you taught him how to plot a story. Little do you know that this separation is a false ending and that you are going to be surprised.

A year passes. It's a hard year in your life, full of loss and sadness, the kind of year that makes a person vulnerable and desirous of smelling the roses again. What's a writer/mother/busy person to do in such times but go on drugs? A shrink hands you a prescription for Prozac. Your depression is stubborn, so pretty soon she has you on a hundred milligrams a day. Suddenly the world becomes a different place. Who knew you could feel so fabulous! Nothing bothers you. You don't mind waiting in movie lines, you can spend hours pushing the swing in the play-ground and running up and down the steps in Riverside Park as your toddler blows off his energy. You easily pass the hardest test of all, weekends with your in-laws. You can't remember what used to bug you about them. They're kinda fun, really. Everything is fun. Who knew?

Then it is spring. Now has the winter of your discontent become glorious through the miracle of the seasons, and modern pharmaceuticals. You love the world. You love everything in it. You take this splendor-drenched frame of mind with you everywhere you go. You take it to the first night of your new writing class. You're thinking this is going to be the best class ever, especially because of RD . . .

Huh? RD? Back for more? So it seems.

Your eyes meet.

And meet.

And meet.

He looks handsomer than ever, but also more himself, less of the resemblance to the movie star now that you are paying heightened, undepressed attention. He is tall, jaw and sinew, and cool. You remember cool, cool was fun, but no one you hang out with traffics in it anymore. They're all fuddy-duddies! RD, on the other hand, is effortlessly cool. He works in film—of course—as an indie producer, but he wants to write stories, he is taking your class to learn to write real stories, how cool is that, and sweet, and ironic, the opposite of many of your students who work in magazines or the publishing industry and not so secretly aspire to write screenplays. He's thoughtful, smart, interesting. You find yourself looking forward to class every week so you can see him. It's stimulating to feel the little buzz you get from him—but in spite of the Prozac, which has lifted your defenses and swept away your sense of guilt, what can happen? All the preventive variables are still in place. Your husband, his wife, your kid, his kid on the way . . . yup, he told you his wife is pregnant. So double the impossibility.

Oh well. Maybe you'll end up as friends. He's a good writer, so you wouldn't have to lie to him about that. You picture meeting in coffee shops for stimulating intellectual conversations. The buzz would be there, but that would only be a side dish, not what filled you up. You begin to think that's really possible—then suddenly he starts acting weird.

Hmm. Whereas he used to maneuver to speak to you for a moment or two after class, now he rushes out. Whereas he used to sit at the foot of the table, directly facing you, as if he were your husband at a dinner party, now he sits in the middle on the side, so you can barely see him. He glares at you when you call on him, and he refuses to do the in-class exercises, often leaving at that time to go home. What happened? What did you do to suddenly have him turn against you? You gave him some fairly comprehensive criticism on his last story; perhaps it was too much for him, even though you put it in a context where you specifically told him that he is talented and his work is good. He doesn't seem fragile, but perhaps you misjudged that. You decide you'll talk to him after the next class. The situation has to be cleared up. He's putting a bad vibe into the room that you can't cope with anymore.

You leave your apartment early on the next class night so you can walk there. You need some time to think before you see him. You head across Ninety-seventh Street and turn right, down Central Park West. At first you are locked down in your own thoughts, but the rhythm of movement in your walk and the balmy air lure you to notice the lovely evening. The trees are pink and fragrant, and so are the girls on their roller skates and in their spring secrets. It's a night for lovers. Well, you had them, didn't you? Somehow, now, years past that time, the lovers fade into the background and you wonder if perhaps it was about the nights themselves more than anything. It is this feeling, isn't it, of gliding through warm air that makes you not want to die. You forget about RD as you stroll along among your fellow spring-sots. You simply enjoy. You are out alone in the world, no husband, no child—a solitary but not lonely person in the weather of possibility. This is the real romance, the love of the world. Now that you are forty-two you appreciate that. Who would want to be younger again? Who would want to go through all the pain of falling in love?

You have all this in mind when you walk into the classroom. RD is already there, bent over his notebook. Suddenly you feel impatient with him. Him and his scowl.

You begin the class. He stands up. You ignore him. He paces the room. You pay no attention but treat him exactly the way the dog trainer taught you to respond when the dog does something wrong—you act as if you don't see it. This goes on for some time. RD is becoming more and more agitated. Why did he even come to class if he can't sit still? He's thirty-three years old, for Christ's sake. Finally, you can't stand it anymore. His wild energy is bugging everyone. You flash him a stern look. He responds by tearing out of the room. Automatically, you follow him. He's bouncing off the walls in the hall, his handsome face stricken, emphasis on the handsome. This makes you even angrier.

"What's going on?" you ask sharply.

He stares at you. Then he steps forward and grabs your arms in his hands and squeezes you toward the center of yourself as if you are an accordion, and he presses and pulls you toward him, his eyes press you, too, and then . . .

He kisses you.

He kisses you.

How long the kiss lasts you couldn't possibly say. A second shorter than forever. Finally, he pulls back and you look at each other, both of you with eyes wide. Then he pushes the stairwell door open and disappears.

You stumble back into the classroom. The students look at you curiously, but not too much so, they don't guess, or know, or care, they're eager to get back to their work. This isn't their excitement. You, however, are completely flustered. What just happened? Did it happen? You touch your fingers to your lips. Yup, there's a residual vibration there; a chord has been struck. It's an incredible feeling, one you haven't had in a very long time, maybe not even since you were fourteen and you first kissed a boy and you didn't know how to do it, you kept having to break away because you felt like you were suffocating. A friend gave you a tip—breathe through your nose. That opened up a new world. You kissed and kissed and felt so tenderly toward that first boy; and you do toward this person, too, for reminding you that your teenage self never really went away, she was merely dormant beneath all the layers of mature behavior and responsibility.

RD awakened her/you. The whole episode moves you in the most sublime and innocent way, even though technically that kiss qualifies as adultery. Your mind rejects the word. It sounds so ugly, and this was so sweet. You feel more fourteen than you did at fourteen. It's a lovely feeling, but your mind is gone. You feel, but you can't think, not even a little bit. The only thing you can grasp is that his stuff is still in the room. You look at his notebook and backpack intently, as if they might speak and explain what is going on. These items, there all alone, are very touching. You keep an eye on them as you somehow get through the rest of the class. He doesn't come back. You don't know if you should take his stuff with you or not. You try to make a reasoned decision about the matter, but in the end act out of a rush of protective ferocity. You'd kill anyone who messes with his stuff!

You are a lioness, and he is your lion, depending on you to hunt for him. Or something like that. Or maybe more like, if you leave the stuff in the classroom, it will get stolen.

As you are gathering everything up, you glance at the open page of his notebook. Your initials are written there—or carved, would be more like it, it looks like he has traced them over and over dozens of times. And they are underlined. You snap the notebook shut.

You take the elevator down to the lobby. Everything is a swirl of sound and color, very trippy. You can barely remember who you are. Aren't you married? Don't you have a kid? It's hard to think. You need air. You head toward the exit and emerge into the balmy soft Manhattan night. You close your eyes and take a breath. When you open them again, you see his face. *The* face. Has anyone ever been more beautiful? Plus, he was *waiting outside*, for *you*. You don't know what to say. You hand him his belongings.

"I'll call you," he says, and runs off into the warm dark.

He does call, the next morning. It's awkward. And exciting.

"So?" he murmurs.

"I don't know."

"Me neither."

"I mean . . ."

"Yeah."

Somehow this conversation is completely intelligible to both of you.

"Why don't you and your wife come over for dinner?" you say, thinking bud-nipping is best.

They come. This is a plan that never works, but you don't know that. You are inexperienced in the world of adultery. You figure out your mistake quickly, however. You know it was stupid the second you see him running up the stairs of your building, carrying a pie. Yikes, what's he doing here? Where you live. With your husband and child. He and they have nothing to do with each other, they are two different parts of you, the twain should never meet. Too late for that, though.

"Hi," he says. His face is tense. Your heart does a gymnastic move. Oy. This was not a good idea. You know it but you can't do anything about it, not even properly think about it, because there she is, close behind him. Whoa. Not at all what you expected. He's so gorgeous and, yes, cool, but she's . . . you don't even want to put it into words. Too mean.

You should have known right then that you were out of your league, that there were forces at play between them that were way beyond you. Instead, you pity him and think he deserves better. You, for example. But wait a minute—when was the last time you thought that about a guy? And how did that end? Right. That's a sentiment that should have you running for the hills. Instead, trouble sits down in your living room. Then your dining room. Then it looks like it is walking out the door, but it doesn't. He leaves, she leaves, their unborn offspring leaves, but trouble stays with you, in the form of longing, yearning, and a bereft heart wrench after he is gone. That is not the result you intended.

This sucks!

He calls on Monday morning. You agree that your feelings for each other are not exactly platonic.

And so it begins. And so it goes—like this: you talk on the phone. You write each other letters and faxes. You tell each other your lives, what matters. You talk about writing. When possible, you meet before class and walk around Central Park. He loves you. He says so. Which doesn't mean anything is going to happen, you both agree, nothing can happen, you're both married, and though you don't feel any guilt about going this far, thanks to the Prozac, you do know you don't want to take it anywhere that would truly hurt your husband if he found out. RD feels the same way. His wife is pregnant, after all. What's he going to do, leave her right before the baby arrives? As far as affairs go, this one is pure. Or purish; maybe not when you're kissing at the back of the Sheep Meadow, or lying on the ground in Strawberry Fields during a storm, laughing at the sting of the rain, your limbs tangled. You wouldn't want your spouses to see the letters, that's for sure. You could claim they were writing exercises, but no one would believe it, unless they were for a class taught by Percy Shelley. You wouldn't want your big feelings to be anything but secret and delicious. You don't want a full-fledged affair, only one that is good enough. Which this is. Right up until it isn't.

One morning, you call him. She answers.

"Oh, you. Yes, he'll speak to you now." She has a sneer in her voice.

That's funny. Or maybe not.

"What's going on?" you say.

He drops to a whisper. "She's upset."

"Yeah, I got that. But why?"

"She saw a letter."

You shiver. "How?"

"It was out."

"But . . ."

The blame kicks in. You tell him he wanted to get caught. He says you're wrong, you're ridiculous, why would he want that? You invoke the power of the subconscious. He gets furious. The fight rages on for an hour or so, with no resolution. It seems silly, all this drama for a couple of kisses in the park. But it's enough that he is forbidden to see you ever again. As it turns out, in the mind of the jealous wife, a good-enough affair is like *almost* in a game of horseshoes. It counts.

You go to your shrink in tears, but she has something more important to discuss with you than the cute guy. She has learned that she has been prescribing way too much Prozac—more than is given for even the worst cases of OCD. Your heartbreak coincides with your going off the drug, and he fades out of your system along with all the lovely lack of inhibition you felt for a while. It's over. Really, it barely was.

Ten years later you can hardly remember what he looks like. You were clearly out of your mind at the time. You very rarely think of him, maybe once every three years. You Googled him when you found out that it was possible to check out old boyfriends that way, and there was indeed a photo of him on the Web, but it wasn't the boy who grabbed you and kissed you in a hallway because he couldn't help it. The picture was that of a working man, a stranger. No one you know.

Sometimes you do think of those weeks, spring in Central Park, the recklessness of attraction, and you know that no matter what rewards time and commitment have brought, nothing can ever be as much fun as that feeling. When anyone asks you if you've ever had an affair, you automatically say no, because really, you didn't. But in your secret heart, where you will always be fourteen, you understand why RD's wife got so upset. It counted.

THE MAN UPSTAIRS

by Adair Lara

⌒~~~This week my husband, Bill, is scorching his shoe leather on Manhattan sidewalks on his annual trip to meet with agents and authors who want to sell cookbooks to his company, Chronicle Books. So I've been seeing a lot of my ex-husband, Jim. He makes roast chicken, reserving the legs for me because he knows I like dark meat. We cozy up on his sofa in the attic and eat it while watching *The Sopranos,* borrowing each other's glasses to try to figure out the remote.

Bill doesn't mind if I see a lot of Jim. He knows it would be hard for me not to, since Jim's flat is right above ours in the yellow Queen Anne Victorian we share in San Francisco. When I'm reading the *Times* in the kitchen I know when Jim's phone rings because I hear his chair scraping backward in his own kitchen as he gets up to answer it.

New acquaintances don't even try to conceal their surprise when they discover that my ex-husband lives above us. It's as if we casually mentioned that a homicidal maniac lives up there. One friend, seeing Jim and Bill in our hallway taking turns jabbing a broomstick at a smoke alarm set off by Bill's backyard grill, said sardonically, "Next you'll have to rent that little apartment in the basement to Bill's ex-wife."

We aren't going to go that far, but I don't blame them. How can you have a permanent bond with someone after you've been married to him? We're obviously passionless people with milksop in our veins. Exes are supposed to slash each other's tires, drunk-dial each other late at night, and poison the children against the other parent, not wander upstairs to see if the other has any red grapes.

I've been trying to decide whether to add that Jim is gay. The risk is that you might say, with that look of having understood everything, "So it wasn't a real marriage in the first place." Of course the two men get along. Does Jim pick out our slipcovers while he's at it?

It was a real marriage, though—complete with sex and kids, jealousy and fights over how to stack the dishwasher and whose idea was it to try living in the country that time?

Jim was my teacher in junior college thirty-five years ago. He was wry, and I'm a sucker for wry. In my first slaved-over paper for his English IA class, on Elizabeth Bowen's "Tears, Idle Tears," I wrote, *This story revolves around Regency Park in London.* He scrawled above that, *I hate revolving fiction, don't you?* He was the smartest boy in the room, and I had always fallen for them, right back to pale-eyed Rodney Dugan in the third grade. A year after I got an A in Jim's class, I moved from the low-ceilinged overheated apartments of Marin into Jim's Victorian, with sixteen-foot ceilings and a grand piano in the living room. In his world, people read the *New York Times* and drank wine over late dinners and had season tickets to the American Conservatory down on Geary Street.

I bought a convertible VW and drove often to Marin to advise my family to buy antiques if they wanted their furniture to be worth anything in a few years. Maybe that was part of it—wanting to escape my working-class hard-drinking background. And maybe I offered Jim a way out of a way of life that had never really sat easily with him, not with that sticky heartland South Dakota upbringing of his. He told me he remembers when he and the other farm boys would go to town on Friday night to meet girls in the hot dusk of Main Street; he knew he was different, that he lived for the moment when the girls went into the glowing rectangles of their front doors.

There were boys, but there were girls, too. A girl chased him into the air force, which brought him to California. Human beings have range.

Jim and I got married, and the kids came along. I pushed Morgan in her stroller along Haight Street while Jim ran behind Patrick on his Hot Wheels as he careened down the driveway beside the Harvey Milk Center. We'd have fun making up cowboy-song lyrics.

He began a small press with the publication of a little history book of mine about the town of Petaluma, an hour north of the city. I can claim some small role in his success, because he listens carefully to my opinions on book projects then makes a killing by doing exactly the opposite. "Nobody wants to read about Mount Tamalpais," I inform Jim with great conviction, so of course he sells out his entire first printing in two weeks.

But it could not have lasted. I was so young when we met that he had to teach me not to say *hunnert* for *hundred* and *acrost* for *across*. He was twenty-one years older, and as the years went by the age difference began to tell. One night he snapped off the radio as I listened to "American Pie," saying he had only a finite number of hours left on Earth, "and I've decided not to spend any of them listening to rock music." I snapped it back on.

And yes, I had begun to need a different kind of admiration than what he gave me in abundance. My marriage was a civilized union that seemed to grow thinner as it stretched into its seventh year. It was not a sterile coupling—far from it—there was the astonishing love for our children, and the physical world we entered when they came: the blood of childbirth, fecal matter, tears, the erotic pump of baby on breast. Jim loved me, needed me, paid my Chevron bills without complaint, and made love to me once a week, always fetching the towel afterward. But he never looked at me; never reached a sly hand under my blouse; never drew me, still trailing bits of broccoli, from the cutting board to bed.

Everything Jim does is permanent. His house is full of antiques, he keeps the same bedspread on his bed for thirty years, he publishes histories, he marries for life. When I told him, he slammed my door so hard the window shattered. Then he replaced the glass because it was his door. When I left, I didn't go far—to a downstairs apartment that Jim rented out, and that I now made him give me for free.

He typed out the Robert Frost poem "Ends" and left it on my table one morning. The poem deals with a breakup, and it ends with a line about how lovers say all kinds of things to each other, but some actually mean what they say.

He did mean what he said, but he had married someone considerably more breezy, more West Coast. I came from a family where divorce was no big deal. "In my family, we marry for life," Jim told me. "In mine, we marry for love," I retorted. "When love goes, we go too."

I was just over thirty. To me then, as now, staying in an unhappy marriage would be like condemning myself to live all my life on frozen ice, floating by happier couples on their tropical islands surrounded by music and the scent of flowers. I was sure that once I had identified myself as unhappy, I had to act on that. In fact, when I'd met Jim at age eighteen, I *was* already married, to a slender dark-eyed lift-truck operator named Mike Lara who could throw a baseball harder and straighter than I'd ever seen, and who had a motorcycle. Getting hitched was easy: We packed plastic tumblers, a change of clothes, and my sister and her boyfriend into the car and followed the predawn highway to Reno, with "Chapel of Love" spilling from the speakers and highways signs flashing by: SHORT MERGES AHEAD.

So I've been married three times, if you count Mike as a real marriage, which I don't. Jim and I had a real one. It was a short marriage, but it wasn't a failed marriage. We produced two new human beings together.

When I left, the bond loosened but never broke. "You should know joint custody works in only ten percent of cases," intoned a lawyer on Montgomery Street, his features shadowed by the bright window behind him. I picked up my backpack and left. It took years to get around to a legal divorce after that, and then we used the same lawyer, a former student of Jim's named Jean-Yves, to file for both of us. The whole thing cost $125, the filing fee, and we had to take Jean-Yves out for pizza afterward, to try to cheer him up. "Oh, well," he said, sounding embarrassed and a little sad. "I suppose that was what you wanted."

I rented various apartments, sometimes alone, sometimes with boyfriends, but I never moved more than two miles away from Jim's house. Once I found a ramshackle apartment right next door to him, so close that from my bedroom I could hear the screeching as he pinned wet laundry to the line and then sent the kids' clothes swaying above the backyard like shadow children. In my kitchen, the kids danced to Madonna and Michael Jackson, and ordered pizza. Patrick had newts, rats, turtles, fish, and frogs. We rented a lot of movies, spent a lot of time going swimming. At Dad's house, they got roast chicken and two vegetables, piano lessons, trips to Europe. The school lunches he made were so much better than mine that I looked forward to the days when the kids would forget them at my house. (I always meant to remind him that I didn't like mayonnaise.)

The divorce was good for me. It allowed me to drink wine on a mountaintop in Maine with David and fly to Tahiti with John and, finally, to meet my next husband in an elevator. It allowed me to climb the masthead at two different magazines and then get a job on a paper. The kids spent half their time with me and half their time with their dad, who also took them after school. Sometimes I'd get messages at work saying, "Your husband called." It surprised my coworkers, since I'd passed myself off as single, but it never surprised me. Jim seemed so much like a husband, always showing up in his Volvo station wagon where he was needed, that it took years after I remarried for me to stop thinking of Jim that way.

After I'd been single for about seven years, I married Bill, a blue-eyed editor with Kennedy hair who rode his bike in the howling gale to the beach on the weekends, read history in the kitchen, and cooked. We moved across the city from Jim into a cavernous rented house owned by Russians, and then came back. My daughter, Morgan, turned thirteen and began slipping out to walk the cold dawn streets with her friends. Jim and I would meet at my house or his and go out looking for her together, slowing down to inspect blond girls in baggy clothing.

It was time to circle the wagons. And by then Bill had convinced me that we couldn't just rent forever, and since we couldn't find a house in the city that we could afford, Jim sold us the flat below him in his huge Queen Anne Victorian near Duboce Park. Jim and his partners had restored it in the seventies, stretching linen on the living room walls and painting the inside walls vivid blue, mustard, green.

It was like coming home. If I walked over to the window, I saw my own children's names scratched in the cement sidewalk. I knew that summer was coming when the boys across the street began sunbathing on their roof, beach towels flapping in the afternoon wind. Morgan and Patrick treated it as one big house. Their friends would ring both our doorbells at once, just to see who came to the door first. Once I heard Morgan tell somebody on the phone, "All of my parents are going out. Can't you come over?" It wasn't long before we all treated it as one big house. Jim walked in unannounced, always calling, "Hello!" but then using his key. Bill and I borrowed bread and ice cream and extra platters from Jim's kitchen so often that we called it the "Jimstore."

Even now, no matter how often I go up there, it's always, fleetingly, like stepping into my own past. Jim never changes anything. Most of the pictures on the walls are of the kids when they were younger than five, because I put them there. My idiotic blue Borsalino from college is in the closet, my photo albums on the living room shelves, my college texts in the attic. I keep my raisins in Jim's cupboard because otherwise I'd eat them all at once. He comes through our flat to stay dry on the way to his own when it's raining.

It can get weird. Once in a fit of housekeeping, I threw out a huge ball of unmated socks. "Oh, I know you did," Jim said when I happened to mention it weeks later. "I found them in the trash. I had most of the mates."

When I got the dog I'd always wanted, a little Sheltie Lassie look-alike, and then accidentally acquired a Russian blue kitten when I bought one for my dad and he didn't want it, our ill-tempered old cat Mike spent the next month under the bed. No creature could ever replace black-lipped Mike in our affections, but we did like the new cat and the new dog a lot better.

I moved his litter box and food and the aggrieved Mike himself to Jim's back porch, pinned a note to his collar, and left. Jim admired Mike. He'd come down to use the fax machine or explain why he had driven our daughter to school again after he promised he wouldn't and then linger to tell me anecdotes about Mike's antics, while Mike himself gazed at me from the kitchen counter with his slate green eyes to make sure I was listening, and then he'd rake me with one remarkable paw when I came too near, to remind me that he was mad about the dog coming to live with us. Jim protested, but then he had protested about our keeping our Ping-Pong table in his attic too, and it stayed there for two years.

Whenever Jim got on a plane, he'd tell our daughter, Morgan, "Watch your mother." I had a tendency to clean out his closets, tossing stuff over the deck to the yard below. Jim hoped I'd given his old vacuum cleaner to Goodwill, "because if so they might still have it." On the other hand, I came home once to find him spontaneously throwing a garage sale and was just in time to keep him from selling that dusty old Borsalino and a lot of books he'd decided I no longer wanted.

Trying to get his Volvo station wagon for a ski weekend not long ago, I reminded Jim that we're a family. He said no. He would have had to lend me his car if I were still his wife, so clearly we'd crossed some sort of line, at least in his mind. (I took the car anyway, of course—it holds more than our Jetta.)

I could have referred him to the *American Heritage Dictionary,* which defines *family* as "the union of man and woman through marriage and their offspring; one's spouse and children; persons related by blood or marriage." But then the dictionary adds that a family is "any group of two or more whose emotional bonds are permanent."

We never talk about our marriage. I would probably not feel right about using his toothbrush now. We are close but never behave in a way that a brother and sister wouldn't. We had to learn a new skill—maintaining distance with someone when you know what makes them cry, what's in their sock drawer, what they told you when they thought you would stay forever.

Oddly, in a way I did stay forever. A divorce that is the end of something can also be the beginning of something—like plants reseeding after a fire.

Our children, now grown, live three blocks away, side by side in basement apartments in a building Jim and Bill and I bought together. The three of us have entered a new phase. Morgan is married, with a three-year-old and a one-year-old. Bill is Faux Pas—he's the stepgrandfather; I am Bobbie (which I chose after everybody, chillingly, tried to hang "Nana" on me); and Jim is Granddad. The three of us babysit, and after dinner we march around the table to the "Jammie Song" (actually Prokofiev's Opus 99) with the girls. And with two twenty-somethings living nearby, we are still coparents, making deals with each other over how much help to give them (meaning, I make Jim swear not to put any more money in their accounts or pay their credit card bills, and he ignores me).

When I see Jim's right hand jammed in his pocket to conceal the shaking of Parkinson's and think how much older he is, I am forced to remember that he won't always be here, that events will overtake our decision to be in each other's lives forever. Meanwhile, we continue to walk in and out of each other's houses without knocking. In fact, when he came down to my office to use my copier, Jim saw this piece on my desk. When I came home, he'd crossed out several lines, then scribbled an apology for peeping: *I was sitting here, and I saw my name . . .*

WANTED HAIR GROWTH
by Patricia Berry

⌒ Recently my husband, Mitch, and I struck a deal. For years we'd worn abbreviated his-and-her haircuts that suited our busy lives, if not each other. Now we would each grow our hair to a length that pleased the other. In the end this pact said far more about the state of our connubial bliss than about our respective coiffures.

The need for a settlement became clear to me the night my husband arrived home with his latest barbershop special. Mitch knows I like his hair best when it has a certain unruliness to it, and yet the sandy brown waves that had flipped deliciously over his shirt collar that morning were gone, shorn to a military length that lay flat and lifeless. The empty billboard between his hairline and collar could have fit the words SEMPER FI in seventy-two-point type. I hated it, as he knew I would.

He shrugged off my protests. "You want me to grow my hair? You know what you have to do."

I did know, and it annoyed me to be under his thumb. Mitch has always preferred the long hair I wore when we met; it was one of the features that drew him to me. Over his simmering objections, I'd been wearing a close-cropped suburban mommy do for a decade now, and I liked how it looked even if he didn't. His own military cuts were about economics, not aesthetics. One shearing every few months suited his thrifty temperament. Although growing his hair out for good would certainly cost him any leverage he might have over me, I doubt he gave a moment's thought to the subject.

Nevertheless, I made an issue of Mitch's stance. Didn't my usually high-minded husband recognize that by asking me to grow my hair he was channeling *Cosmo*-like, How-to-Snare-a-Man values? And while we're at it, what message was this sending our three young daughters whom we were raising, we both hoped, to be independent thinkers who can make their own choices? Assuming they were paying attention, wouldn't they want to know why Mommy, their role model, shouldn't wear her hair any way she wanted to?

The real problem lay elsewhere, though. I did not appreciate having to give up something to have my way, least of all something that could be construed as an invitation.

Truth was, I had grown comfortable in my role of mother and less so in my role as wife. The last thing I wanted was to give my husband any . . . ideas.

Even if holding up my end of the bargain would have the desired effect of making me more desirable, the notion of growing my hair at forty-five made me shudder. Fashion magazines may tout the recent trend toward longer locks among the long of tooth, but it would take a greater power than *Vogue* to convince me that when hair passed my shoulders after a protracted absence, I wouldn't look more like Willie Nelson than Cindy Crawford.

But then there was the unmistakable fact that while leafing through the newspaper over coffee and cereal that morning, my husband had been adorable to me. I easily might have leaned over his shoulder to help with the crossword puzzle and twirled one of those wandering strands around my index finger. Now I'd have to wait another six weeks or more to touch him that way, and I was pissed.

The time had come for compromise. Mitch would leave his waves intact and I would grow a ponytail. The only way to have my desires met, I had finally grasped with scissor-sharp clarity, was to meet his.

Duh.

Hearing and, more important, granting my husband's wishes wasn't always such a teeth-gnashing ordeal. Even in this case, the initial act of compromise was a means to pleasing myself—a quid pro quo arrangement—not an act of compliance. But once I gave in to it, the deal became less about the hair and more about getting back something that we'd neglected: our mutual attraction.

Like most men I know, Mitch likes things simple. Asked what his ideal woman looks like, he hesitates to answer. ("Do you really want to know or are you baiting me?") After a step back, he takes the bait. She's wholesome-looking with a sense of fashion but not too edgy, he tells me. She wears body-conscious clothing and natural-looking makeup. And she has un-fooled-around-with hair, the longer, straighter, and blonder, the better. (Apparently, she also owns a pair of calf-high white go-go boots that she brings out on special occasions and wears with little else. He ducks. Until this point, I bear some resemblance to this ideal, but there are no go-go boots on my shoe rack.)

Wholesome. Youthful. Sexy. To my husband, those three words are synonymous.

Lucky for both of us, there is a photo of me that Mitch says illustrates his point. I am twenty-eight or twenty-nine and dressed up to meet a group of his college friends for the first time. I'm wearing a clingy black dress and sheer black stockings, and I am looking at the camera, which is tilted at an odd, upward angle. My hair, wheat blond and blow-dried to ruler straightness, is loose and falls below my rib cage. Somehow this fuzzy old picture captures his ideal woman, although she is going on twenty years younger than me.

Nineteen, to be exact. It's a long time to be with one

person. And it's impossible to imagine our relationship not evolving over that time, for better and for worse. But for all the growing that goes on in a long marriage, there are things that get left behind that, I've begun to realize, are worth retrieving.

When we were new lovers and had an abundance of disposable time, we could glide through our evenings and weekends in the pursuit of simple pleasures like jogging together in the park, napping in spoon formation on the couch, and preparing dinner for two. I'd watch with affection the way Mitch hugged the sofa pillow like a stuffed toy as he slept or screamed at the TV when his beloved New York Rangers let go of a lead. Throughout our downtime, there were moments when one of us would simply gaze, soaking in the other and thanking his or her lucky stars. Once caught, there'd be a smile, a wink, maybe a kiss through the air between us. Those little moments were plentiful and, I think now, not so little.

So bursting was I with my good fortune, I arranged for a group of my girlfriends to join us for ice-skating so they could check him out. Mitch and I hadn't known each other long and here I was showing him off, confident that he was the One. I wanted them to see Mitch at his sexiest: on hockey skates flying along the ice, now skimming backward and weaving around the other skaters as though they were stationary objects. He was appalled when I admitted the setup, and a little flattered, too, I'm sure, though he would never admit it.

My hair was a useful prop. Mitch could turn an hour of detangling after my evening shower into foreplay. We'd sit, Mitch behind me, on the bed or floor, and he'd wrap his legs around mine. Comb in hand, he'd work through small sections of my hair, stretching the task. We'd talk about work, our plans, and, yes, our dreams. Once finished, he'd kiss my neck, and lovemaking would usually follow.

He had strong feelings about starting a family as soon as I was ready. That would be a while. To me, babies meant the end of what I considered a perfect arrangement. I couldn't imagine that children wouldn't steal something from us.

Which is what they're supposed to do, of course. We sleepwalked through the early child-rearing years, piecing together the "just the two of us" part with date nights and occasional getaway weekends. But it wasn't the same. The opportunities for romance lessened, and so did my desire. For a while there, I would have forgotten about our love life completely—if Mitch hadn't been there to remind me.

I had stepped from the confident forward march of a woman on a career path and very much in love with her husband smack into the uncontrollable whirlwind of parenthood. After our second child arrived, my editing job disappeared, and staying home to raise our family made sense, especially since we were planning on a third child. From chasing toddlers to keeping up with the increasingly busy schedules of older children, I found myself caught up in their lives and virtually disengaged from my own. I volunteered in their schools and managed their sports teams, taking stabs here and there at a writing career but only when I could fit it in. I was finally going to write my novel, but then I'd throw obstacles in my own path, agreeing to host a fundraiser or prepare Thanksgiving dinner for thirty or, frankly, to do whatever anyone asked me to do.

No wonder I had no energy for lovemaking; I had filled our days—and our nights—so effectively that there wasn't room for intimacy even if I had wanted it, which I'm pretty sure I didn't. Frustrated, Mitch watched from outside the tornado as I went around and around, scrambling to catch hold. His reaction was to stay the course, to be as best he could the voice of reason and sanity and the arbiter of what is just enough activity and what is simply too much. Often, he would ask me not to overschedule our weekend so that we could just hang out with the kids. I'm ashamed to say I took his sane approach as a weakness, as though whirling around like mad was a good thing.

When you are young and eager to love and be loved, physical intimacy goes hand in hand with expressing your feelings for another person. Mitch pointed out that the frequency of those expressions dropped precipitously after we had children. Romantically speaking, years four (when our first was born) through thirteen (when the youngest turned five and finally stopped crawling into bed with us) of our marriage are a blur. It's not as though we didn't have sex for ten years, but there was, on my part, something mechanical and vaguely obligatory about it. One thing I do remember is Mitch's heartfelt fear that if we didn't use it, we most certainly would lose it, and didn't I realize how terrible that would be for both of us? To be honest, I don't think I did. Mostly I just wanted to keep my head above water through the daytime hours so that come bedtime I could crawl between the covers and feel some relief. Unfortunately, it wasn't the type of relief my husband had in mind.

Looking back, I don't know why my interest so utterly waned, unless it was that in creating this crazy life for us, I thrust on him a role that made him less attractive to me: that of the heavy. I did accuse him once of terrorizing me. I think he had asked if I could get the kids to clean their rooms or something equally innocuous. In having to rein me in, he lost a little of his boyish appeal and charm.

I could not have been all that attractive to him either, what with my frantic pace, verbal lashings, and frequent use of the queen of all spousal punishments, the silent treatment. I appreciate now that Mitch was a patient man.

As if to slap an exclamation point onto my feelings—or lack thereof—I cut my hair. It was just after our second daughter was born, and I was training for a marathon, my get-back-in-shape-after-baby regimen. With all of the running I was doing, I could actually see my cheekbones again. I'd always wanted really short hair, but having a round face, I considered myself an unsuitable candidate. Now, twenty pounds lighter, I grabbed the opportunity, and the scissors. I loved running my fingers through my pixie cut and having them pop out the other end without pulling a strand out from its follicle. I was hooked.

Mitch was mute.

I didn't realize it then, but cutting my hair emphasized something I was gradually cutting out of our marriage. He certainly would never say I was less attractive to him. Mitch is no dummy; putting such feelings into words surely would have ended sexual relations for good. But I'm sure it crossed his mind.

The mind and body can only do so much. I have tried with uneven success to find my limits, only to discover that balance happens not when I am trying to reach those extremes but when I operate closer to the center. I don't know what happened to bring me nearer to that core, but I believe my marriage is the healthier for it. Perhaps I had to spin around and hit a few walls before I had the sense knocked into me, but over time I have come to understand where I need to be.

And wherever it is I am, Mitch is with me. Our love life is here too, thank goodness. It's not what it used to be, not now that we are closer to fifty than thirty. But it's fair to say that the romance, felt especially in little but not insignificant moments, is back. Where for a long while there was frustration and avoidance, now there is something resembling harmony and closeness. Funny how a little compromise can lead to even better things.

And then there is the hair. Our eyesight isn't what it was, so I don't see so well his receding hairline, and he conveniently misses the fact that my hair is also thinner and going gray. (If I quit highlighting, I'd be grayer than he is, but I'm not ready for that dose of reality.) No longer symbolic of a power struggle, our mutually longer hair is a nod toward our attraction to, and affection for, each other.

It's work, this long hair. The wash-and-wear days are long gone. Without a hair dryer, I look like Willie. Then again, a dab of hair gel, a little makeup, and a pair of stretch jeans, and I think I can even turn a head or two. Most important, I've turned his, and that, after all, is what this whole deal is about. The bonus is now I can twirl his unruly strands to my heart's content.

PRETTY YOUNG THINGS

by Steven Rinehart

⌒⌒⌒ I think I was a sophomore at the University of Hawaii when I realized that college professors actually did get to sleep with their students. Of course I had seen *Animal House*, but those teachers were old folks, actors, potheads, and what have you. I was in love with an English major who had just started to notice me, and as we sidled and maneuvered our way into a relationship I discovered that my sweetheart had been dallying with her English professor. I don't know if they actually had sex, but he wrote her poetry, and as a result she spoke of him dismissively, the way I imagine Maud Gonne might have spoken of Yeats ("he's so smitten, the little drunken dear").

This professor apparently had a wife back home in Boston, or an ex-wife, or a fiancée. I didn't know exactly what was going on, but I figured out quickly that making me jealous was tremendously arousing to my girlfriend, and I was for that reason happy to play along.

I remember odd bits of behavior from both of them—the appraising looks he gave me in class, followed quickly by condescension, surly scribbles, and marginalia on my deft and economic three-paragraph dissection of "The Waste Land"; her overly dramatic locking of the desk drawer before we laid down on her bed, fully clothed, to thrash and argue and, usually, dry-hump our way to sweaty torpor. I didn't give a rat's ass what they wrote to each other, and I didn't think for one second that she was being taken advantage of by him. Mostly I felt sorry for the guy. I mean, I never wrote her poetry, for crying out loud.

Ironically, four or five years later I found myself in graduate school sharing a house with three poets. There were even poets in the house next door, something I thought was exhilarating for the first week and a half. It was one of the poets next door, though, that I'm still reminded of when I stumble across, by sheer horrific accident, a copy of the *American Poetry Review*. Peter had been a housepainter in Boston who had applied to our graduate program specifically to study with a visiting poet of some national stature. He had been accepted, and spent his first few weeks writing, drinking Guinness, and falling in love with a fellow poet, the lovely Betsy. Unfortunately for my friend it took almost no time for the visiting poet to very publicly declare Peter's work third-rate and then to steal away the beautiful

Betsy for an even more public bacchanalia. Peter returned to Boston poorer, wiser, and saddled with student loans; the poet went on to further acclaim; and Betsy was honored the following year with poems about her and then, quickly afterward, by her, in the *APR*. Ah, graduate school.

I'm older now than both of those professors were when those events took place, and while I don't teach full-time, I am an adjunct at a prestigious private university. I'm also married—eleven years. My mind is still fairly sharp, and I'm in decent shape. I teach creative writing in a program that appears to be mostly women—this semester only three men are seated around the table with me. But this year is just like the previous six or seven; the young women, while being for the most part intelligent and, in several cases, quite lovely, are not the slightest bit alluring to me.

I'd like to think it is just my superior morals at work but there is something else going on here. Somehow I've fallen on the gray side of a serious generational divide. While I find much to admire about my students' work, their personalities, and in a few cases their moral universe, I generally find them to be physically . . . well, distasteful. Not disgusting, mind you, just mildly off-putting.

I can, and will, immediately give a lot of credit for this to my wife for the maintenance of her undergraduate figure, which, I like to remind her, is nearly exactly what you'd find on an undressed Saks mannequin. She's a perfect size 6, or whatever a slender six-foot redhead measures out to be. That's tremendously helpful. But more important, she sports no tattoos or odd piercings. Her clothes are generally clean (I know, I wash them). Her waistbands remain in the general vicinity of her waist, not strangling her ass from either side. Her nails are usually pink, not blackened. She reads, owns no iPod, speaks from the middle of her palate and not from back near the uvula. She votes. She moves gracefully and can, in a pinch, swing dance. She's a great shower date.

I can also credit the modern political climate in academia, where a program of male castration appears to be fairly complete. Few of us drink anymore, fewer smoke. Nobody really publishes what previous generations published: big, bawdy books filled with transgressive sex. Hell, we don't even teach those books anymore.

The closest I get to giving my students the "we're grown-ups now so why don't we read like grown-ups" treatment that I received, with generous servings of Henry Miller and Philip Roth, is assigning a half dozen Mary Gaitskill stories; great stuff, but nobody really wants to have sex after putting one down, at least not without a mask. No mysterious Mona, no Portnoy, no *Goodbye, Columbus*. We meet with our female students with the office door open. We socialize minimally, and with small groups. We bring up nice things about the boys in the program, give them props, try not to publicly demean their rather pathetic confessional fiction. We were them once; somebody saw something in us. Give them a chance, girls.

But I don't need these rules, regardless, since most of

the time I spend alone with students is devoted to figuring out what they're talking about. Any time the conversation veers away from deciphering my scrawls on their manuscripts I find myself wondering at what point my country had been spirited away and replaced with a reality show starring attention-challenged Generation Y xenophiles. (Did I ever spend a half hour trying to convince one of my college professors that it was a good graduation plan to sell jewelry, write novels, and work at a record company?)

But I am a writer of fiction, an imaginative sort, so my mind travels every now and then to that what-if place, and I think back to previous semesters. There was the dark-haired Hispanic girl who stretched a lot in my direction. There's the one actress a year who wears a white wife-beater T-shirt with a black bra underneath. But where would we have gone? Dorm, hotel room, tiny apartment with roommate? I never had the nerve to buy a *Playboy* publicly much less be seen skulking around a girls' dorm in my Dockers. Garp did it with a babysitter in a car, if memory serves, as did his wife. But I live in New York City, and getting the minivan out of the garage for a tryst somehow seems tragically inept, even if the seats do magically disappear into the floor.

Perhaps it's my libido—is it tired, or still intimidated by that rather dramatic (to me) vasectomy a few years back? Friends of mine who have pondered vasectomies sidle up to me when they find out I've had one.

"Does it have any effect, you know, on the whole thing?"

"What whole thing?" I ask innocently.

"You know, is there any difference?"

"What, in the product?"

"Yeah."

"Well," I say, "now my wife and I can both fake orgasms."

They tend to go pale at that point. They don't get around to asking about the pain, which, quite honestly, never quite went away, at least psychically. I still react to anything moving quickly in the vicinity of my waist with a knock-kneed spasm resembling an NHL goalie facing a power play.

But the simple truth is that these females are, to me, children, and therein lies the rub. (Especially in these post-Monica days, where childhood for young American women appears to end around thirty. It does make one wonder if we were all better off when Eva Marie Saint could coo to a silver-haired Cary Grant, "My name is Eve Kendall, I'm twenty-six and unmarried. Now you know everything.")

I've always been drawn to older women; at least I was well into my thirties. I was still in high school when I saw *Shampoo*, and that kicked off a fairly serious Lee Grant fixation (I saw *Charlie Chan and the Curse of the Dragon Queen* six times; don't get me started on *Portnoy's Complaint*). I spent the better part of my twenties stumbling through haphazard affairs with women over forty. I have no idea what they saw in me; mostly I spent those years in a drunken, self-pitying haze.

A confidante of mine told me that those women, mostly

single but in one case married, were using me for decoration, which never quite made sense to me. How decorative could a six-foot-three-inch depressive be? I remember one cocktail party in graduate school where the male friends of my then paramour attempted to talk to me, size me up. One of them, a kind person, asked me about my writing. I told him my current project was a novel written from the point of view of a cat.

"Really," he replied, nodding. He was the kind of guy who would have looked good nodding with a meerschaum pipe.

"It's plotless," I said. "Kind of meandering. Like *Tristram Shandy,* except with a cat. Have you read *Tristram Shandy?*"

He had. I hadn't, so I quickly asked him what he did. He owned a wine store, so I queried him, apparently quite rudely, about why *claret* couldn't be pronounced like any other self-respecting French word, like *ballet.* "You could charge more for it," I said. I was told that I later attacked him for dissing Theodore Dreiser.

That woman kept me around for another week or two before sending me out for a corkscrew and locking the door behind me.

As I write this it occurs to me that perhaps we've all grown up. Not just those of us born at the tail end of the baby boom, but everyone. Maybe no college professors sleep with their students anymore. It wouldn't surprise me. The world has become a more careful place since I was young, or perhaps that's just the way I see things. My twenties were filled with nuclear nightmares; we didn't expect to get old. Now that I'm staring mortality in the face, having buried not only a parent but friends, the only plausible answer is to invest close to home. Lust globally, perhaps, but love locally, extremely locally.

The last Lee Grant film I saw, the one that ended my obsession, was *The Hijacking of the Achille Lauro*. Ms. Grant played the wife of the doomed Leon Klinghoffer, and her performance was devastating. I couldn't tell you if it was actually good or not, but the effect on me was instantaneous—the old magic was just gone. I couldn't picture those cheekbones anymore, those bangs, without seeing Karl Malden pitched into the froth, hearing her heartrending screams. But it didn't matter; the nineties were almost upon me, and big changes with them. I had sobered up, mostly. I was planning a big move to New York City, but the thing I couldn't have known at the time, the thing that seems so simple now, was that just eighteen months after that film came out I was to meet my wife, all six-foot, red-haired, exquisitely boned inch of her. She had just gotten through a divorce, and a postdivorce love affair; she was, she said, ready for a grown-up and for some reason thought that grown-up was me.

I wasn't, of course, but she must have seen something— the forty-five-year-old me creaking around behind my thirty-two-year-old self, perhaps. I wouldn't doubt if she saw the safe bet I would turn out to be—broken, not in the china sense but in the mustang sense, ready to be at peace, tired of the callow and loutish barking world of bars and the interminable dress-up games that passed for a social life. Maybe she saw that I'd scared myself enough with the drinking thing, the drug thing, the jail thing, and had no interest anymore in chasing experiences.

Whatever the reason, I'm forever grateful that she possessed that penetrating sight and have to keep reminding myself not to take her for (Grant)ed. Not five years ago she participated in a photo shoot at the magazine she worked for, and somehow a picture of her fell into the hands of one of the young heartthrob actors from *Dawson's Creek*. It was a very good picture. He apparently badgered the editor or agent or whoever for her identity. And I know exactly what he was thinking, the punk.

But as far as I'm concerned, he ought to find a woman his own age. I did, and I recommend it highly.

LIKE A BUNCHA VIRGINS
by Helene Stapinski

At first I blamed the husbands, because that's how I operate. My girlfriends are my peeps, my comrades, and the husbands, well, they're just lucky to be married to my girlfriends. That's how my thinking went.

So when I heard that my friend Jancee's husband was watching porno behind her back, actually hiding tapes around the house, I grimaced and helped her call him all sorts of appropriate names: pervert, sicko, deviant.

Then there was Maureen, whose husband was away all the time, whether on business or out with his friends. She complained over the phone about how lonely she was, and to make her feel better, and because I really meant it, I called him names too: Ingrate. Insensitive lout. Jerk.

A few months later, Ellen called me crying and told me

she thought her husband was cheating on her. Rat bastard, I said.

Then Nancy called. Her husband too was having an affair, she thought. Though she wasn't one-hundred-percent sure. She had found e-mails on his account to a woman who appeared to be his mistress. That son of a bitch.

The topper was when my friend Elliot called to tell me he was leaving his wife and young son. Maybe his timing was just bad, coming on the heels of all my conversations with my aggrieved girlfriends. But I lost it.

"What do you mean, you're leaving her?" I shouted into the phone. I didn't call him a bad name, but he knew it was coming, just on the tip of my dirty tongue. So he jumped in with his defense: "We haven't slept together in years," he said. He had tried to get his wife to counseling, he explained, but she'd refused. And, well, he'd gone and met someone else. He was in love. And the sex was great.

How could I blame him? Sex was part of the marriage contract, as far as I was concerned. And besides, it felt good. Woody Allen had once said that even bad sex was good. I didn't understand: Why would Elliot's wife refuse to have it? Sex was one of those things in life—one of those basics—that we should be grateful for. Like food and wine, kids and real estate. Sex was a good thing, especially if you liked, or loved, the person you were having it with.

I remembered back to the time before my husband and I were married, back when sex together wasn't just good but also constant. Back then I had trouble walking, we did it so much. The guy knew what he was doing, and we fit pretty well together, physically. I'm only five feet tall, and he's considered on the small side for a guy. (Heightwise, not sizewise.) Most important, he never quit until I was satisfied, even when I told him not to worry about it. The guy was determined.

When he asked me to marry him, I worried, probably like most people about to take the plunge, if I could spend the rest of my life with him. I had a professor in college who said that marriage was one long conversation. Deep down inside, I worried that maybe we'd run out of things to say to each other someday. I worried that I would run out of things to say to whomever I married. I mean, a lifetime! Wasn't that crazy?

But the one thing I never worried about was whether or not the sex would always be good. It wouldn't always be new, but it would be good. I knew I'd always be attracted to him, and that even when I wasn't in the mood, he'd put me in the mood. I figured I'd always say yes to sex with him, and would always be happy that I had.

So after thinking about it, I forgave Elliot for leaving his wife for another woman, a woman who not only was willing to put out, but who enjoyed it.

While I was thinking about Elliot, though, a terrible reality dawned on me. I realized that my girlfriends—Jancee, Ellen, Maureen, and Nancy—had something awful in common. Not that their husbands were undeserving monsters. But all of these friends hadn't had sex for many months, some for a year or two. Not because their husbands weren't delivering the goods, but because they refused to answer the doorbell.

They were exhausted from the kids. (Okay.) They were afraid of getting pregnant again. (Lame.) Or they just, well, they just didn't want to. (Really lame.)

It suddenly became very clear why Jancee's husband was watching porno. Why Maureen's husband didn't want to be around her. Why Ellen's and Nancy's husbands were fucking around, or at least considering it. They weren't gettin' it at home.

Now these women, remember, were my peeps. My comrades. Women I had grown up with. One of them had told me in kindergarten how babies were made. (I had laughed and told her that that was the stupidest thing I had ever heard.)

Ten years later, we were in a school courtyard and she was explaining to me, in graphic detail, how to make out with a boy. She had been the first girl in seventh grade with boobs, and she knew how to use them. She, naturally, explained second base to me. And third. And eventually, how to round home in style.

Some of these friends had been sex kittens in college. Ellen had worn sexy lingerie and high-heeled feathered bedroom slippers, just for fun. Maureen had shown me her vibrator once. Jancee was so sexually active, she actually had crabs sophomore year.

What was going on with them? Was it simply middle

age? But I was middle-aged and I loved to have sex. I could safely say that I liked having sex even more now than when I was younger. I knew exactly what worked for me and had no qualms about directing my husband in new and exciting directions. I used to be shy about talking in bed, but no longer. I was confident and horny. And when I wasn't horny, my husband convinced me that I was.

Being married for eleven years had made him an expert in the business of pleasuring me—and me him. I knew that in any profession, it took ten years to become a master. And we had become masters of each other's bodies. It was one of the fringe benefits of being married: lower taxes, shared living expenses, and his being able to find my G-spot in less than three seconds.

It wasn't like we were doing back handsprings in the bedroom, mind you. Or swinging from the chandelier naked. The kids were in the next room, after all. My husband and I just had really good sex, quietly, regularly. Or sometimes great sex.

We did it about once a week, sometimes more, sometimes less, depending on child-induced sleep deprivation. All my sexless friends were around the same age as I was, forty-one, and had kids around the same age as my kids. But they were much too tired, they said, to do it anymore. Much too young, I said, to live on the memories of past orgasms.

I soon realized that it wasn't just sex my friends were avoiding. My friends hardly ever went out with their husbands alone. My husband and I had a standing date to go out once a week, every Sunday night, to remind us how much we liked each other. And good, sometimes great, sex usually followed.

But I could no longer share that information with some of my closest friends, friends who started to sound more like the nuns who had taught us in grammar school than the bad girls I knew they were. I felt like I had been dropped into some horrific inverted *Stepford Wives* plotline, where once-happy, previously satisfied women refuse to have sex with their mates and simply complain all the time. Was I the only married woman on my block having sex?

It got to the point where I felt bad even mentioning my dates to them, never mind our sexcapades, since all they did was complain about their own husbands. When they complained, I just nodded, or grunted. And I did something I had never, ever done before in my life. I sided, silently, with their husbands.

When I was growing up, my mother had spoken of sex as if it were a chore, something she'd rather not do, but had to, like a dental cleaning or washing the windows. I was different, I knew. And my generation was different, I had thought. We weren't old enough to have burned our bras, but we had listened to Madonna as teenagers. We marched for abortion rights and vowed never to change our names. We had had multiple partners and anal sex. And we talked about it.

I wondered lately if my friends were really liberated.

Or maybe too liberated, if such a state exists. They were liberated enough to tell their husbands to buzz off when they came near them with a hard-on, a luxury our mothers never had—mothers who simply lay back and tried to enjoy. It had been their duty to give it up every so often for our fathers.

After my initial confusion, I grew angry with my friends for turning into old, boring, middle-aged ladies (ladies who, by the way, had gone and changed their names). I felt like my friends had been day-trippers, feminist sex kittens while it was fashionable, but were now minivan-driving Little League moms with no libido. With the procreation out of the way, it was time to enjoy sex for sex's sake. Wasn't it?

Once my anger faded, a sadness started to creep in. I missed the old days, when we talked about our sex lives, about who liked bondage and who didn't. About the best way to give a blow job. About new and exciting methods of birth control. (Remember the sponge?) Those vibrant sexual friends seemed to be lost to me forever, bound together by their new vows of celibacy. I felt like an outcast. I *was* an outcast. But I wasn't about to join their no-sex club. Sisterhood had its limits, after all.

I decided to do what any superfreak girlfriend would do. I would help them get it on.

I encouraged Maureen to get a babysitter and go out for a romantic dinner with her absentee husband, thinking it would certainly lead to other, more interesting positions.

She complained bitterly that they had no money for a babysitter. But she had just bought a Sub-Zero refrigerator, for chrissake. They had money. Who was she bullshitting? A new, sleek kitchen appliance was just more important than a sex life.

No. Money wasn't the issue. The more I talked to her, the more I realized that Maureen didn't seem the least bit interested in hanging out with her husband.

So I moved on to Nancy. I encouraged her to try to talk to her husband, find out why he was e-mailing that other girl. She flew into a rage about how she wanted to but every time the topic came up, she nearly grabbed a kitchen knife and stabbed him in the neck.

Not wanting to be accomplice to murder, I moved on to Jancee. I suggested she watch porno with her husband. She looked at me as if I had grown a third ear in the middle of my forehead. I shrugged and gave up.

It was at that point that I realized that these women, and many of the men and women I knew, didn't really like their spouses a whole lot, and in retrospect, maybe they never had. Some had married for financial stability, others just to have kids, still others simply because they were asked, or because they had reached a certain age and wanted to register for Limoges china. Many of the men I knew treated their wives as if they were their mothers, asking permission to go out with their friends and sulking when "Mommy" said no. Where was the equal partnership? Where were the soul mates?

The men my friends lived with—the men they were supposed to be having sex with—were not their friends. There was no dialogue. Very little joy, save what the children provided. Barely any companionship, even. They were not on the same wavelength, sometimes not even in the same radio market.

All they had were preconceived roles, an old faulty mom-and-dad model that they had grown up with, one that had been passed down since the Stone Age: Me hunt. You take care of children. Me build fire. You cook meat. Except for the Design Within Reach furniture and mortgage, they may as well have been living in a cave.

I had had that same exact outdated model as a kid. But where they had embraced it as scripture, I had rejected it, wholeheartedly, one hundred percent. No, thank you, ma'am. No fucking way. I was determined to marry someone I could have that lifetime conversation with. Someone I wanted to have sex with for a long, long time. A friend and lover. And, after much thought at the time of that proposal long ago, I had decided he was the one I could talk to for the rest of my life. And have sex with for eternity. (Or at least until we were too old to bend our knees.)

Now, don't get me wrong. Our relationship was—and is—no paradise. We fought. We still fight. God, do we fight. Once in a while I throw things, barely missing his head.

We are survivors of an extramarital affair, an affair that threatened years ago to destroy our young marriage, but actually strengthened it. (Our sex life even improved after the confession, something dirty and forbidden amping up the wattage.)

The affair also left us both wounded, of course, and horrified and clinging to each other, committed to never, ever doing anything like that again. We are confident there will be no midlife crisis for either of us—at least not one that involves cheating. Maybe fast cars. Or a Greek isle solo vacation. But no more screwing around. At least not with other people.

At the end of the day, after the yelling, and the throwing things, and the ugliness and the therapy and the fantastic sex, at the end of it all, we are still old friends. Old friends who like each other, who like to talk, who like to go out to dinner and chat, and who really like to sleep together. Who love to sleep together.

Maybe we were just lucky to have found each other. Maybe we are deluded. But all I know is that I want to sleep with my husband while most of my friends have reverted to virgin status. Maybe it's just some awful phase they're going through, a phase that I hope will pass by week's end. But until then, I'll keep all my sex stories to myself.

TOO MUCH INFORMATION
by Lian Dolan

〜 Here's my wish for you: I hope you are all having down-and-dirty, ooh-baby-baby, crazy sex seven nights a week and twice on Sunday. Really, turn down the lights, crank up the Luther Vandross, and proceed to a tantric state with your spouse/partner/young lover. May you go at it like bunnies until well past your prime. Just do me this favor: Do not tell me about it.

I don't want to hear the blow-by-blow over coffee or read about it in the *New York Times* in some well-meaning column on love. Same goes for buying your soft-porn memoir or stumbling across your sex tape on the Internet. If you're tempted to tell your BFF during a cell phone call in the elevator about what happened with your webcam, could you wait until I get off on the seventeenth floor? Your mother called them private parts for a reason.

I miss the time when regular folks whispered about carnal acts instead of shouting about them in a Starbucks. Sex is great, super, but I think the details should be kept between the two, or three, participants. I am not a prude; I read *Cosmo* during my mani/pedi like everybody else. I devour all those medical and pseudopsychological studies about sexual attitudes and frequency and hang-ups. I once bought a copy of the *Kama Sutra* as a bridal-shower gift. See, I'm not uptight. I just don't understand discussing the whole making-whoopee thing in a group setting. Never in my life have I had brunch à la *Sex and the City*, rehashing the performance of my man the previous night. Sure, I've had brief conversations with my girlfriends about some plumbing basics, but when the conversation veers into specifics, I'm out.

Frankly, it's embarrassing, and it's nobody's business. More important, it's not polite to share the intimate details of my relationship with an entire table of diners. It violates the trust of the other person involved, and nobody wants to eat breakfast links after a discussion about erectile dysfunction.

Once, over coffee and bagels, an acquaintance that I had identified as a potential friend blamed her postpartum exhaustion not on the crying baby or the nursing at night, but on her ravenous, hairy-backed husband. Seems he wanted it at least once, sometimes twice a day and has for years!

No newborn in the house was going to stop his desire, she exclaimed. And while sympathizing with her plight, I was simultaneously scanning for exits. I wanted off that friendship train. I hadn't even memorized her home phone number yet! Why would I want to know about how many times a day she does it? Now, when I see the couple across the soccer field, it makes me cringe just thinking about the details I never asked to know, especially the hairy back.

But I am just one small boat in a turning tide. I can't seem to get away from other people's sex lives. Social commentators offer multiple theories about who or what is responsible for this current tell-all environment. You can point the finger at everything and everyone from MTV to MySpace.com, from Bill Clinton to Paris Hilton, from *Friends* to *The Bachelor*. Ads are thick with sexual innuendo; acting careers are built, not destroyed, by home sex tapes. Bookshelves are littered with titles like *Confessions of a Naughty Mommy*. (Writing a book like that means never having to be the PTA president.) The other day I was reading an essay by a sportscaster, for goodness' sake, and even he had to tell me about where, when, and how he and his wife conceived their first child. Enough. My vote for who is to blame for this ubiquitous desire to divulge mating habits? Kathie Lee Gifford.

Remember when Kathie Lee would chat it up with Regis in the morning? There she was—a churchgoing, holiday sweater–wearing, suburban mother—telling Regis and the whole country, in no uncertain terms, that she and her stud muffin husband, Frank Gifford, had done it the night before. She would wedge this little detail in between an anecdote about potty training and another about recording her new album of Christmas songs. Kathie Lee and her husband were having sex on a Tuesday night in Greenwich, and she wanted to let us all know. Like we were wondering? It was shocking and tantalizing and a little icky.

Sure, we'd always been intrigued by the sex lives of movie stars and the cast of *Melrose Place* (hey, it was the early nineties), but Kathie Lee was the first to make it perfectly acceptable for normal people to talk about the secrets of their bedrooms in a public forum. And not just any normal people, but normal, middle-aged people who you'd never suspect. Husbands with receding hairlines and jumbo mortgages. Classroom mothers driving minivans and selling real estate. These sorts of characters were not the romantic heroes of yore. Sure, hearing about the exploits of attractive twenty-somethings holds a salacious, fantasy quality. It's a reminder of what used to be. Remember when we were well toned and full of elastin? Oh, yeah. That's a good escape, vicariously reliving those days. But the image of two average parents doing it? No, thanks. I am a parent and I have parents. In neither case does this conjure up a pretty picture. Just because it's about sex doesn't make it sexy. And yet, Kathie Lee's on-air disclosures opened the floodgates. Soon all sorts of people, including total strangers on a plane, wanted to tell you about their fertility treatments or ex-husband's proclivities. Deliver me.

Talking about sex, particularly my own sex life, is not in my gene pool. I come from a long line of repressed Catholic women who never uttered a single word about sex. The only birth experience we ever discussed was the Virgin Birth. Having the original Madonna as opposed to, say, the Material Girl Madonna as a sexual role model can be a little intimidating. And though I grew up surrounded by my mother, many aunts, dozens of female cousins, and four sisters, the atmosphere at our house was not exactly the Red Tent. More like the Red Muzzle. We were isolated, all right, doing the dishes in the kitchen, but we talked about the magic of scalloped potatoes, not the wonders of womanhood. Even still, as the youngest of eight kids, you'd think I might have heard a few helpful hints over the years, but no. Like Carmelite nuns, my older sisters appeared to take a vow of silence in all areas concerning sex.

It could be that my sisters were talking to one another but not to me. The six-year age gap between my next closest sister and me was the gulf that divided the *Mod Squad* generation (them) from the *Brady Bunch* generation (me). It was the seventies, the height of the sexual revolution, but you'd never know it at our house in suburban Connecticut, at least from my vantage point. I was too busy reading *Harriet the Spy* and taping Leif Garrett posters to my walls to observe any kind of revolution. I had no idea that people from Fairfield County had sex lives until I saw Ang Lee's *The Ice Storm* and Kathie Lee opened her mouth on TV, both events occurring well after my formative years. Now, in retrospect, something may have been going on in the bedrooms of our bedroom community. Mainly gin and tonics, but perhaps a little sex, too. I suspect my sisters were whispering something tantalizing behind closed doors and under cover of their Joni Mitchell albums, constantly blaring. But all I heard was *Ladies of the Canyon*, no juicy details.

Perhaps my sisters weren't forthcoming because we all had the same unenlightened education in this area. My mother handed us all The Book, which focused on the nuts and bolts of "the reproductive system," which is what we called sex in our house. That was followed by The Movie, shown in the fifth grade, which emphasized hygiene and how to secure the sanitary-napkin belt, an ancient precursor of the fanny pack. Though the complete contents of The Book and The Movie are foggy in my memory, I definitely do not remember any suggestions such as, "When you sleep with somebody, be sure to tell as many people as you can about your night of passion, particularly if it involves the kitchen table." Apparently, that piece of advice made it into other books.

After I saw The Movie, I approached my mother.

"Mom, we saw The Movie today?"

"Oh. Do you have any questions?"

"No."

"Okay then, let's go watch *Merv Griffin*."

That was my one and only conversation with my mother about sex. But that's all I needed. I could figure out all the rest from Judy Blume, a copy of *The Happy Hooker* I found under my sister's bed, and my friend Kiki, three years older than me and much more informed. Kiki's mother was a Francophile; maybe that had something to do with her superior grasp of all sex-related terms. Kiki was the one who explained just what exactly Mrs. Powell's retriever, Whiskey, was doing to the Whitmores' standard poodle, Daisy. Whew, that was quite a day. It took me several years to get over that revelation. I couldn't really translate it into human terms until my sister Sheila took me to see *Coming Home*, a wildly inappropriate movie for a twelve-year-old.

By the time I hit junior high and then high school, I gravitated toward friends with the same limited information and experience. Girls with good grades who played field hockey and took jazz and tap. Listening to Prince's *Dirty Mind* was the naughtiest thing we ever did. We couldn't get dates, so there really wasn't an opportunity to "explore our sexuality," as people say now. Back in the day, conversations took place face to face, so talking about the sex we weren't having was just pathetic. We couldn't fake it as easily as kids today, hiding behind online personas and virtual dates, so we didn't even try. Sure, we liked boys and occasionally they liked us, but not enough to stop our other interests, so let's move on. Really, re-creating the Go-Go's videos in our bedrooms was far more entertaining. We were pleasantly in a bubble, not prodded by pop culture to grow up too soon.

Fast-forward twenty-five years, and here I am, a mother with two kids and a husband. Along the way, I internalized the idea that sex is healthy and part of a loving relationship, but it is not a proper topic at a cocktail party. Must have been that Emily Post on the bedstand next to *Are You There, God? It's Me, Margaret.* Believe me when I say that I am even less tempted to talk about my sex life now. But that does not seem to be the case with my peers.

Take a look around at the plastic surgery and the belly rings and the tattoos on grown women and it's clear that my generation is not taking aging well. And the older this crowd gets, the louder they seem to be yakking about sex. "I'm fifty and I'm having the best orgasms of my life," I heard a woman at the hair salon say in a stage whisper to her stylist. I'm no medical expert, but I don't think revealing this sort of intelligence to a guy named Damon in a yellow silk shirt actually stops the aging process. (It probably grosses Damon out, too.) But I have no doubt that the woman in the highlight foils thought that it might. If I can talk about it, then I can still do it. And if I can still do it, then I can still breathe. Intellectually, I know I should applaud any woman who has the cojones to make such a statement. But it skeeves me out. And that is the crux of my dilemma. Very happy for her orgasms, would just prefer not to hear about them.

Since the early revelations of Kathie Lee, the genre of let's-talk-about-sex confessionals has blown wide open. Everybody wants to share their hot private lives. Now we have to hear about the sex lives of 'tweens (but not my kids, right?) as if the notion that 'tweens have sex lives is perfectly normal. Add Jack LaLanne's daily dose of nooky to the list of things I do not want to discuss. And if that's not uncomfortable enough, sexual dysfunction is just as popular a topic of conversation as sexual function. I defy you to consume any media over a given hour and not hear the words *vaginal dryness* at least once. I know it's a serious medical condition, but isn't that what doctors are for? Do we really need the anchors of the local news tackling that subject?

I host a radio show six days a week with ample opportunity to pull a Kathie Lee. Please, the producers beg me, reveal something tawdry. It's great for ratings. And it is tempting because it is such an easy topic. Sex automatically gets everyone's attention, as opposed to new prescription drug legislation. And on the radio, no one can see the toll that gravity has taken on your tush—good for both anonymity and the gross-out factor. Still, I resist. My husband nearly left me when I mentioned on air that he was red-green color-blind. Can you imagine if he heard me go on and on about his—well, never mind.

Frankly, I'm at the point where I'm just grateful. Grateful to have a husband with a nice head of hair, two healthy kids, a house, and a job I love. I'm grateful for bagged salads, Spanx, and the resurgence of candlelight for home use. I'm grateful that every once in a while, my husband will put on Roxy Music and the years fall away when I hear "Avalon." And what happens after that is nobody's beeswax. Let's just say I'm grateful for that, too.

Growing up, I often heard the expression, "Discretion is the better part of valor." Well, I say, "Discretion is the better part of sex." Doesn't keeping it a little bit more secret make it seem a little bit better, particularly at this stage of life? We don't have to take our attitudes about sex back to the Dark Ages, but I wouldn't mind if we turned off the light occasionally.

Just Like Bogie and Bacall

by Shaun Assael

Every so often, I'll peek into my wife's side of the medicine chest, not to be nosy, but because I've cut myself shaving and need a Band-Aid, or some such thing. I don't find any pills that Liza Minnelli would want to pop at a party or vials that were recently featured in an investigative report on *20/20*. Just attractively packaged creams and emollients. Still, they seem to exist in their own universe, known to a clubby few.

For the purposes of research, I made notes one day on the labels of just two. One offered itself up as being luminiscing (though I'm fairly sure that's not a word) while the other advertised itself as flaw-fixing. I scratched my head as I considered the definitions. I suppose that if I really wanted to know what they meant, I could have asked my wife. But that would have been weird, plus no good can ever come from putting the words *flaw* and *fixing* in the same sentence with her. I could have also asked those flaxen ladies with frozen smiles who patrol the aisles of department stores. But they give me the creeps. And, anyway, it seemed like too much work. So the mystery of her creams went unsolved, adding a precious layer of intrigue to our Home Depot medicine chest.

When you've been with the same person as long as I have, I've discovered, it helps to find mystery in your lives where possible. After jostling for sink space at six in the morning and grumbling through the car ride to the station, a good-bye kiss on the lips feels like a power pact between two busy people rather than a revelation. It's not until I'm on the train platform, staring at my wife pulling out into the morning, that I begin to marvel at the woman I've been with for twenty-seven years.

Having a relationship built around mystery is a wonderful thing, but it's not for the fainthearted or the languid. For one thing, it takes a lot of energy. You have to be obsessed enough to want to find out the answers to the questions that the unknown poses. (Where does her smile come from, and how does it spring to life so easily? Why does she insist that the title of Steve Miller's "Jungle Love" is really "Boogaloo"?) Most people I know—and not just married people—don't have the time to put into such things. As a result, the mystery in love tends to be for the very young or the idle rich, leaving the rest of us simply mystified.

This isn't wordplay—okay, it is, but hear me out. Finding mystery relies on your being inquisitive. Being mystified depends on your being willfully ignorant. If you spend your days worried about the Chinese oil markets, or whatever else has nothing to do with your darling, then the odds are good that something she does will catch you by surprise. An argument will ensue, and each of you will accuse the other of misunderstanding. That's not the soil that the intriguing, beguiling love—you know, the Bogie and Bacall kind—tends to grow in.

As it happens, my wife has always been good at being mysterious. She was that way when I first met her as an NYU frosh. I was sharing a dorm room with five guys, one of whom had spent the prior year living with her and four other women in a rental home in Tucson. Having come to New York to visit relatives, she stopped by, wearing a gauzy shirt that didn't quite reach her waist, torn jeans with flower patches, and sandals. On a walk through St. Mark's Place, then a haven for the punk scene, she flipped off those sandals and waxed on about desert campfires, magic mushrooms, and the works of mystics like Carlos Castaneda.

She took my breath away, and it wasn't long before we were living together in a Tucson house with beads that hung instead of doors and a basement where a prior tenant had left a pentagram. (Don't ask.) Two years after that, we were both back in New York, sharing a tenement over a gun shop.

For a brief, very brief, time, I tried buying her clothes. In the early eighties, there was the red leather miniskirt with the big black zipper that got worn exactly never; the Valentine's Day negligee that elicited embarrassed giggles; and, Lord help me, the fake sheepskin jacket that managed to horrify both her mother and our cat. After that, I started giving electronics and jewelry, which was useful in the years when we lived in a tenement that regularly got robbed but today represents a quiet concession to the fact that I won't get within a blast zone of Bloomingdale's.

All the while, she smiled happily and continued to dress stylishly without ever appearing to be a slave to style. How, I don't know. I stay away when the closet door closes and sounds of scuffle sweep through our home. What goes on between her and her wardrobe is her business. I assume that, as with all art, it comes with its own pain and sacrifice. The not knowing is good.

Our twenties were a blur (hey, it was the eighties), our thirties about trying to make it with a kid in the city. My wife opened a toy store. I joined the NASCAR circuit for a year to write a book. For the first time, we were apart more often than not; me traipsing across the country with my racing friends, her focused on making a small business profitable. It wasn't until our forties—after she'd sold the store and I was on to my next book—that we realized we'd come through separate, life-changing experiences, closer than ever. How'd that happen? I'm still not sure; it's part of the mystery.

I don't consider myself to be mysterious at all. I work all day, and when I'm done, I hate talking about it. Even when my work is interesting, I grumble and groan. You know those housewife comics who joke about guys who don't like to answer questions, or do so with monosyllables? That's me. Does that make me an enigma? Hardly. It makes me stubborn and lazy. If there are times when I'm intriguing, I don't know it. Which is another difference between my wife and me. She has a deeper, more nuanced palate of moods—logical one moment, stubborn the next, and insouciantly girlish when the time is right for fun.

Maybe it's for the best that we don't share that aptitude. Two mysterious people in the same relationship wouldn't work anyway. An invisible moving force needs a stationary one to slam into for it to take shape. Two moving forces that keep orbiting can do so indefinitely. Try raising a kid like that, much less making life-and-death decisions, like whether to order Thai or Pizza Hut.

There is one topic we have started to talk about lately that I wish we could keep a mystery: plastic surgery. Let me say at the outset, I'm in a weak position opposing the idea. Surely, my wife has a right to look and feel younger. Plus, every guy wants his wife to look hot, right? Well, yeah, but . . .

If you've spent any time in a Dallas shopping mall, you understand that surgically preserved hotness really only comes in three basic varieties: sharp businesswoman hot, perky soccer-mom hot, and hooker hot. This covers everything from the wife who just made law-firm partner to the one who'd jump at a chance to star in a Ratt reunion video. The problem isn't just that I can't imagine which group my wife would fit into. It's that all of them seem so, uh, off the rack. Plus, I've seen too many people with their skin pulled back. They look tense to me, as if the act of turning back the clock has left them tightly wound.

When I look at my wife's face, I can see all the things we've done together etched in her gentle folds. (Note to aspiring wooers: the following phrases were rejected for the previous sentence: *crackling creases, rolling riverbeds, hard-earned age lines.*) That is art to me. It's the canvas of having invested time in someone. Sure, I'd still love her if she had her face worked on. But I'd feel like something was gone. Something I couldn't get back. Some mystery I could no longer uncover.

Okay, okay. So my wife has had one thing done. I won't tell you what, because it's not that big a deal. It was done because it had to be done, and that was that. So let it go. But I notice the difference, especially in those quick-flash moments when I catch her and remember what she looked like when I met her. I worry that plastic surgery would add to the differences that I'd silently catalog.

I've heard the slippery-slope argument. What about going to the gym? Isn't that bad, too? Like I say, I'm in a weak position here. I don't know where to draw the line. All I know is that I want to wake up looking at the same face that I fell in love with, not a simulation.

The same face that, however familiar, is still revealing things to me.

I think she feels the same way about me, though I wonder what she'd say if I wanted to get cheek implants or any of the other things that men seem to get when they become suddenly, sadly, petrified that women aren't looking at them. But I suspect that the whole issue would be obscured by a general feeling that there must be some reason, other than her, that I wanted to do it. And that alone would make it more trouble than it's worth. But even if that weren't the case, why bother? Just as two mysterious people are too much for one relationship, the same is true of cosmetically repaired ones. Have you ever seen them walking down the street together? They're always looking to see who's looking at them, rarely looking at each other.

I'm spending a great deal of time looking at my wife these days, and it's a good thing. In my twenties, two letters could sum up my interest in her body. But as the years pass, I find myself lingering over places that I used to hurry past. Her neck, her shoulders, her wrists. Her fingers while she types. Her forehead when she furrows it. I'll catch myself looking at each, amazed at how they flow and move and add up to something special. In quiet moments, I'll give each some attention. I think it surprises my wife when I do that. Because after the fact, I'll catch her staring in the mirror, examining her wrist, or shoulder, or neck, wondering what that particular body part did to deserve a shout-out.

I suspect I've made her happy because she'll come back to bed quietly, and with a smile. Maybe, in that small way, I'm mysterious, too.

Whatever it takes. My guess is that the next thirty years are going to be fun. Because I keep adding up the things that I'm finding to be intrigued about, and there's no end in sight.

Mystery doesn't come easy in a relationship. But it shouldn't be left to the young or idle rich. I mean, why should they have all the fun?

THE UNKIND CUT
by Mazek Fuchs

There are three men with vasectomies on my otherwise typical suburban block, and the word around the neighborhood is that if we are ever invaded by another cul-de-sac, our side is toast. This particular joke followed hot on the heels of another one about how, thanks to Dr. Snippy, our subdivision shows a statistically significant decrease in chewed slippers and humped legs.

Sensing something already on the subject of vasectomies? Either veiled tears or their first cousin surefire jokes are never far behind when the name of a medical procedure rhymes with such a fundamentally frightening phrase as "Where's the rest of me?"

Talk about an unfortunately opportunistic rhyme. Vasectomy—where's the rest of me?—a turn of phrase that is less poetic than the sort of broadside to the gut that produces instant tears.

Well, it makes me squirm to see you cry, but first things first. Let's get those jokes behind us. Don't think you're the first to ask, for example, if before my own little twenty-eight-minute, thirty-two-second festival with the urologist, I sang baritone one last time. And hold the knee-slappers about how I will be reincarnated as a capon, or castrated rooster. I'm not much for either early rising or foraging for seeds in a pen, so I'm not laughing. Which doesn't mean you are free to ask if I will live out my present life in a demoralized, vegetative state. Or as a member of the Vienna Boys' Choir.

Neil Rothfeder, who got a vasectomy at twenty-six (no, not as an outpatient on an Iowa pig farm—he's heard them all too) after his fourth child and never looked back, acknowledges that any concept that makes male skin crawl brings the collective mind down into the gutter; in this case, cracks about barnyard surgery and ensembles of sopranos. Dr. Robert Stine, a fifty-two-year-old psychiatrist who had a vasectomy after child number six, agrees: "When it comes to the penis, you are just not supposed to cut the thing. It's like purposely denting your car."

The thought of a vasectomy always had all the charm of a firetrap to me. But at thirty-six, and with three children already, I developed the operatic anguish that an accidental pregnancy of twins would give me five children and an early grave, at which I'd still be getting delinquent notices from colleges and wedding halls. I began to look at men who could be my dad and who had young children and thought, There but for the grace of a vasectomy go I.

I am not the sort of new age guy to sing "Kumbaya" while swaying; my nuts are my favorite material possession. But my wife, who I do think the world of, had been through three difficult pregnancies and the same number of train-wreck deliveries. And it wasn't like she had a scheduled C-section for her final delivery, where we could have thrown in a tube-tying for a minimum amount of extra fuss. Birth control had always been in her wheelhouse, not mine—yet there I was, living in mortal fear of more children. It was time to start thinking.

It did occur to me that having a vasectomy might be money in the bank of goodwill—and that it could yield certain dividends. But my main realization was that we had enough kids. And that, comparing the options, it was my turn.

In fairness to the lame jokes, any form of birth control that effectively began with castrated sentries guarding the harems of emperors does warrant some latitude in the humor department. Even when taking a scalpel toward a patient's scrotum, never in itself an act of improvisation (let's hope), many urologists say men are cheered and calmed by a bit of improv. If humor is what is needed to take a constructive look at what might be the only area of male sexuality where the chance at basic understanding is squandered by silence, I guess I can allow some groaners throughout. As Groucho Marx once said: "Those are my principles. If you don't like them, I've got others."

After all, even erectile dysfunction, the second-to-last frontier of shyness on the male sexuality front, has become a marketing and cultural touchstone. But who is the Hugh Hefner or the Bob Dole, the proud face of vasectomies? I'm not quite a Dole or a Heff man, but it would have been great if in my own indecision and raging fear, I had such a role model, a Michael Jordan of the vas, if you will, to help me decode my feelings. And decide, by example, what to do. The true irony is that such was the limit of my understanding that just to hear some pompous celebrity, so far removed from the circumstances of my life, sound off about what I should do would have been an advance.

While no Michael Jordan, Dr. Stine is a willing cheerleader. He describes his vasectomy as, ultimately, a form of tender mercy. "I had six children, and the vasectomy allowed me to continue having sex without birth control, which I could not abide and barely used—obviously, with six children." Considering that the tying of a woman's tubes is more invasive, expensive, and holds more medical risk than this male alternative, Dr. Stine says it is beyond reason that the percentage of vasectomies has not risen in the past two decades.

The Centers for Disease Control, Planned Parenthood— they know that the vasectomy, done under local anesthetic, never wins any popularity contest, and its use will not rise if it remains the only area of sexuality that turns men circumspect, if not green. Afraid to get the unkind cut? Well, slap yourself back to normal and let's take a look at the simple procedure, which has always brought to the fore complex questions.

I certainly had an armload. First off, if I lay down on that gurney, would I rise the same old tiger I'd always been? Might my effort be just the sort of plus-sized gesture that canonizes me in the eyes of my wife so that I get laid forever after with more frequency than a swinger on European holiday? What happens if there is an earth tremor during the procedure? Even without tectonic-plate shifting at just the wrong moment, will I be marred or maimed in any way? Would my beard stop growing? (I don't have one, but you get the point.)

Problem was, even my internist, who had to refer me to the urologist for insurance purposes, gulped when I broached the subject.

"Why would you ever want to do that?" he asked.

I told him about the three kids I already had to send to college, and he answered: "I don't know how you're even going to manage two."

With that passing as hand-holding and answer-giving, I knew I needed more. Somehow, somewhere, I needed to talk to a member of the few, the proud, the snipped.

I knew of only one place to turn, which was to a former marine down the street named Augustine Cardeli. Auggie, as he is better known, has five kids and figured a vasectomy was the least he could do. He promised me that the procedure was an easy hurdle, despite, in his case, an extra-chatty nurse that nearly drove him to distraction as he tried to set his mind deep into the no-pain default mode he had learned in the service during Vietnam. He was astounded by the amount of gauze involved too. But he promised a free feeling afterward that was undocumentable in the history of men. Sex without a sliver of thought about birth control or mouths to feed. It sounded intriguing enough, and I had myself down as a definite maybe.

What almost scared me off was my brief glance at the history of the procedure, a scary look back if there ever was one.

The last time vasectomies were in the public eye, it was courtesy of preachy hippie-dippie sorts in the seventies who tried to popularize a gold-plated vasectomy lapel pin. This innovation made the Edsel look like design and marketing genius. The vasectomy lapel pin was to be worn by men in bars to identify themselves as neuters and attract or at least put at ease the mind of potential partners.

Never mind the fact that your sperm count was never tested before you put on a pin. Or that anyone who preens about a vasectomy to that degree in public (unless it's in a book) deserves never to get laid. Anyhow, needless to say, the vasectomy lapel pin had a shorter shelf life than even the puka bead. And this was a step up from earlier times.

Remember those sentries? The poor bastards were usually castrated in the true sense of the world. Often their testicles and even their penises were cut from them. Same goes for the sopranos of all those jokes. There is evidence that there was even a eunuch singing in the Vatican choir as recently as the early portion of the 1900s. Throughout that time, men were still being castrated to improve health (they never heard of Robitussin?), make them feel younger (affairs with coeds obviously hadn't been invented yet), and to avoid passing on genetic diseases (that is just sad, no joke there).

The first modern vasectomies were performed in the late 1800s. Despite all the legends and misunderstanding that's still attached to the procedure more than a century later, very little was involved, even then. Through two separate incisions on either side of the testicles, the vasa deferentia, a pair of tubes through which sperm travels right before getting mixed with semen, are tied, cut, removed, burned, or all of the above. Still, before the sixties, the procedure was used more for enforced population control and punishment than anything else; it was rarely undertaken voluntarily for birth control purposes until women's equality came into popular focus.

These days, the procedure is also done semi-noninvasively, with a small hole poked in the scrotum instead of a slice. Either way, there is no scarring, and most men are cleared for action within a few days, although birth control needs to be used until semen is tested, usually within two months' time. Erections are the same and ditto for semen, save for the absence of microscopic sperm—which are invisible to the human eye to begin with.

⟨⟨⟨

Kim, a child of the sixties, who asked for anonymity because of the personal nature of the vasectomy's effect (it led to a marked improvement in her nooky rate with Joe), was after her husband to get a vasectomy for years. He dawdled for a decade, then finally did it, though, in a bit of irony, when he was fifty—and Kim forty-six. Noting Kim's proximity to menopause, which would make the issue of having an accidental baby later in life moot, Joe balked. Even his doctor had a qualm. He called the prospect of the unkind cut "a permanent solution to a temporary problem."

Joe and Kim were caught in the cross fire of the doctors, with Kim's gynecologist pointing out, with some outrage, that the two had enjoyed an active sex life for two decades, during which Kim had been responsible for birth control. A long history of breast cancer meant that she had to forgo the birth control pill, which meant a diaphragm, a messy device that translated into chronic urinary tract infections.

On top of that, Kim had been pregnant five times, miscarried three times, and delivered two children by cesarean. She had no symptoms to suggest that menopause was in the near future. Why not Joe, Kim's gynecologist pushed.

The essential key for the Joes of the world—and this

is no easy hill to climb with your wife—is to figure out whether your marriage circumstances are ever going to change, in the form of a younger woman who wants babies. This could mean divorce. Or your wife's untimely death. Either way, it's not an easy subject to broach over a casual glass of wine.

But it is an essential question. Lauren Corrado speaks for many other eligible, beautiful single twenty-six-year-olds when she says that if a man she was dating sat her down to tell her he had been snipped, it could become a sticking point. The question of whether or not he was willing to get a reversal, much more involved than the original procedure but an option with a decent chance of success, would stand as a major test.

In the case of this particular Joe, that was not a worry. Any way he sliced his life, the math worked out the same. Picking up children from the bar or bat mitzvah circuit at age sixty-four did not appeal, nor did sitting sun-dulled in the heat of a college graduation past seventy. He visited a urologist and waited the requisite thirty days (longer than you do for a handgun in some states) to make sure he wasn't being coerced.

"Coerce is a funny word, but I digress," says Kim. In preparation for the big day, the couple, parents of two college-age children, bought several bags of frozen peas, the same thing I used to help mold ice around the area that had to heal. They walked around the Central Park Zoo, their old stomping ground when their children were young, and the message was clear if bittersweet: That portion of their life was done.

As for the next portion, Kim waited with Joe until a nurse brought him in to the procedure room and when he came back, the patient was not, as she puts it, "too wobbly."

For Joe and many others, the procedure is surreal but involves nothing that even remotely rises to the level of pain. For Dr. Stine—and me—there was a single brief moment when we wanted to poke our urologists in the eye. When handling this visa deferential, our doctors apparently tugged on a nerve. Not fun. But in the interest of full disclosure, I have to tell.

Joe emerged so chipper that he insisted on driving home, which Kim knew meant he was still feeling like his normal tribal king self. But first, God bless him—in fact, the very moment the hospital doors swung open—he asked to fly to Cleveland to go to a Browns' game with his best friend from college.

The question was plotted and rehearsed; he had picked his moment with forethought. But what was she going to say?

Joe left, and soon he and Kim were back in business— with a twist that links them to the dozens of others I have spoken to who live in postvasectomy land. From Mr. Rothfeder to Dr. Stine to Auggie and on, sex, even when it was in no complaint territory to begin with, improved.

Gone were the gooey spermicides. The damn diaphragm, the disruption of birth control, the horrors of the condom, also became relics. And on a deeper level, Kim is quick to point out, Joe's effort soothed some low, simmering resentment. With the children out of the house and all these new factors in play, their sex life flourished. With only one adverse reaction, a side effect that I regrettably share. None of us has been able to eat frozen peas again.

I'm honestly not going to get into any scorecarding of my own love life. Suffice to say that when people ask me how the vasectomy has worked, I always give them a sales pitch—which means, at least, that I'm that same tiger I always was. It is incredible, in fact, how curious men are about vasectomies, and since I have written publicly about the procedure before, I always get questions, whispered and more up-front. One day, I might try to make a buck from it all and hang out a shingle as a midwife for vasectomies. I'll talk you through it and wipe your brow for a price. On second thought, you couldn't afford that price.

THE PROCEDURE TO
END ALL OTHERS
by Peg Rosen

⌒⌒"Life begins at birth" has always been my mantra, whether I've been on my way to a voting booth or managing my own fertility. Why then, at this point in my life, am I hesitating for a minute about what I might *DO*?

Why is the idea of aborting a pregnancy made within the loving, secure bounds of my marriage so upsetting? After all, I had exercised my constitutional right once before, back in my twenties. Is this embryo any more or less of a life than the one I chose to purge from my body so many years ago? No, it's the death of potential that's clawing at me—the idea that I'm erasing the possibility, the glimmer of a child who would share the same dimples, curls, and dreams as his (her?) brothers. A real child made from love versus an embryo made during young-boyfriend sex.

Thirty-seven days and no period. I crack open an EPT and hold my breath. I wait for the little window to flash my fate. Am I pregnant? Am I perimenopausal? For a woman of forty-two, both are possibilities.

Each erratic month leading up to this bathroom drama has driven me nearly to distraction. Since adolescence, that familiar stain would arrive every twenty-eight days come hell or high water—except for three pregnancies, two of which delivered to me two beautiful boys. But over the past year, every cycle has ended in a question mark. Never able to tolerate birth control pills and distrustful of diaphragms (that other pregnancy was achieved while using one), I have for years patched together my own birth control regimen involving spotty use of condoms and some careful timing.

Sometimes, I am right on schedule. Sometimes, and ever more frequently as I march through my forties, I find myself counting and recounting the days in my Filofax, anxiously trying to will my period into being, wanting that reassurance that I wasn't, wasn't pregnant.

Ironic that when facing my first possible pregnancy almost twenty years earlier, I wasn't nearly as frantic. Yes, I was single and had just split with my boyfriend. Yes, I was scraping by on eighteen thousand dollars a year as a copywriter and could barely take care of myself, much less a child. But my thinking never went that far. When the test stick turned up positive, the pregnancy itself—the fact that my body was afflicted with "it"—was the matter to be dealt with. I knew exactly what I would do. If I'm not mistaken, I found an abortion clinic in the Yellow Pages. I tearlessly told my close girlfriends and my ex, and didn't bother swearing them to secrecy. In my mind there was no scandal. There was nothing to hide. I marched in there on the scheduled day, read *Goodbye, Columbus* in the waiting room, and exercised a right I felt boldly entitled to.

Now the stakes are different. I stand in this house, in this life. I feel torn in two. The very prospect of terminating a pregnancy, the same love-drenched miracle that gave me my sons, makes me want to weep. And yet, the idea of having another child brings me to my knees. It has taken six or seven years for me to emerge from the fog of early motherhood. My work is pretty much back on track. I no longer force myself to gulp down meals because a baby needs to be nursed or a toddler soothed. And sex? During those early years, I was barely even in the room. I have since journeyed back from sexual spectator to participant, and am on the cusp of becoming a player. I actually want sex.

I knew I was done with babies the moment my youngest emerged from my body, healthy and outrageously alive. But it took a few years for me to acknowledge the end of my reproductive life in any concrete way. Deep inside a very scary part of my soul, I worried and wondered about the worst kind of what-ifs. What if something happened to one of the boys? Was it obscene to even entertain the idea that a child was replaceable? Eventually I took the leap and emptied out the attic. Not a shred of baby evidence remained, save for a few knitted sweaters and caps that will someday be unearthed for my own grandchild, whose mother probably won't deign to dress her newborn in some dusty relic of another mother's journey.

Getting sterilized—a harsh word, but exactly what I intend to do—is a much bigger step. It takes those thirty-seven long bloodless days and the gut-quivering prospect of having to decide what I would do if I have, indeed, conceived. In the bathroom, I collapse onto the toilet seat and weep, genuinely sob, with relief when the EPT informs me I won't have to face that agonizing choice. Determined to make it so that I never have to, I reach for the phone, dial my gynecologist's office, and inform the receptionist that I must have my tubes tied.

"When would you like this done?" she asks politely.

"This afternoon. But if that's not possible, tomorrow morning."

She checks the book; a week from Saturday it will be. I open up my Filofax to the twentieth of March and squeeze the word *Tubes* in among the scrawled notes for 10 a.m. baseball practice, 11 a.m. birthday party at Chuck E. Cheese, and 3:30 kids' cut with Stephanie. I scribble, *Get mom to babysit* in the margin.

Over the next ten days, I receive all kinds of reactions. From my parents comes unflinching approval. Surprising in one sense because they are generally first to plant the seeds of doubt, regardless of what decision I've made. Not surprising because my dad is a urologist and has always sung the praises of vasectomies and tubals (though neither he nor my mom ever took such steps). My mother-in-law, on the other hand, is nonplussed. "Why something so extreme?" she blurts over the phone. I explain how I don't want any more babies, how I don't want the anxiety of worrying about an unwanted one. "But why so final?" she begs. "Why not?" I answer back, knowing full well that she, too, goes straight to the dark side and harbors the same what-ifs as I do.

From my friends I hear, ad nauseam, "Why not Paul? You're the one that had to deliver those babies! You're the one who spent two years breast-feeding!" I don't need them to tell me that vasectomies are also a whole lot less invasive. My response is calculated and reasonable, at least as my emotionally tapped-out mind sees it: Paul is three years younger than I am with decades of fertility stretching out before him. If I were to get hit by a bus (which is the kind of scenario I regularly mull over in my head), I'd want him to remarry. And chances are his new wife, perhaps younger than he, would want to have a child. I, on the other hand, am in the waning years of my fertility. If Paul was to die, there's not a hair's chance I'd want to—or, ironically, even be able to—get pregnant again.

"Don't do it for me" is Paul's response as he lies in bed next to me and listens to my phone conversations. I haven't even broached the subject of a vasectomy with him; he can't get blood drawn without becoming faint. I also know that he hasn't thought a wink about the realities of terminating an unwanted pregnancy, even though he wants another child less than I do. To him, and probably to most men, the whole issue of missed periods and monthly anxieties is part of the feminine landscape. A once-in-a-while hysteria that usually resolves itself quietly, evidenced only by a casual mention before bedtime and some crumbled tampon wrappers in the trash can. I know too that, for fear of being selfish or out of just plain obliviousness, Paul hasn't even considered how much more fabulous his orgasms will be when he doesn't have to put on a condom or pull out on the brink.

Just as my head hits the pillow one night it hits me: the real reason I'd taken this on myself. I want control. In a sexual life blessed with the freedom of choice, I want to make the final one. In the most literal sense, I feel dutybound to tie up my fertility on my terms.

We leave the house just before dawn on Tubes day. With the kids still in bed and Grandma on guard, it was the closest Paul and I have come to a daytime date in years. I rib him about who really has the balls between us, granting him one last chance to go under the knife instead of me when the doctor calls our name. He rues the fact that he forgot to bring the newspaper and will probably be stuck reading back issues of *House Beautiful* while I'm in recovery. We are still talking up a storm when we take the elevator up to the seventh floor of an anonymous office building and swing open the doors to the gynecological surgery center.

The thick silence of the room jolts both of us out of our bubble. As we settle down on a floral sofa by the window, I take a look around. Across from me, a young woman in sweats nervously fills out forms while her—girlfriend? sister?—twists her long black hair into a braid. In the corner by the door, a goateed guy in his early twenties is sound asleep on the couch. Over to my left, a well-dressed woman in her fifties clicks her cell phone closed and quietly begins to cry. The faces may be different, the surroundings far cushier. But I am intimately familiar with this place. The gynecological surgery center is, essentially, an abortion clinic.

Why am I so startled? Wouldn't it make sense that tubals and terminations would both go on at a place like this? I guess I somehow assumed that women who need abortions around here head into Manhattan or Newark or Jersey City, to a clinic with gritty linoleum floors and naked plastic seats, like the one I visited so many years ago. In this cozy womb of the tristate suburbs, where five-bedroom homes and supersize SUVs celebrate fecundity, it's easy to overlook the fact that even here, some pregnancies aren't wanted. And to this cushy-couched office, in this anonymous building, just minutes from the stroller-trafficked Short Hills Mall, is where, I realize, the quiet masses come.

Twenty minutes into an ancient *Oprah* magazine, I hear my name. I give Paul's hand a squeeze and disappear into the back, where I'm presented with the standard surgical paper uniform. As I stuff my hair into the chalk blue cap,

knot the plastic belt of my stiff gown, and slip my feet
into slippers, I recall having changed into the same elegant
outfit once before. That time, I was taken to a room where
other blue-gowned patients sat listlessly around a table.
"This is a condom," announced the nurse who greeted us,
holding a Trojan up in the air. "This is a diaphragm," she
said as she hoisted up her other hand. I sneered, thinking
about what little good that fucking diaphragm did for me.
I expected the other girls—some looked younger than sixteen—to echo my impatience. But I registered only bore-
dom on their young faces. Duh, Peg. Most of the souls
who went to that clinic hadn't bothered with such stuff.
That's why they were there.

I am jolted back to the present when a nurse pops her
head in and tells me it is time. She gently ushers me into the
OR, where I'm helped up onto the table and eased into the
spread-kneed position so emblematic of the female fertility
journey.

"Is this your first time," asks a voice from somewhere
down around my feet. It is my past percolating to the surface again. Memories of my abortion, buried twenty years
deep, come flooding through me for the first time ever. I
remember craning my neck to see who could be asking
such a question and spotting a cute dark-eyed guy with
longish hair peeking out from under his cap. My face must
have echoed my astonishment, because the dark-haired
guy who turned out to be the anesthesiologist quickly
covered himself. "You'd be surprised. Some girls are here

pretty often. They basically consider this birth control."
I started to shiver. While waiting for the clinic doctor to
make his entrance, the anesthesiologist and I got to chatting. He told me his favorite book was *The Cider House
Rules*. Of course. He told me he was Catholic. That he
only moonlighted at the clinic, and that his sister would
have killed him if she found out. I mumbled some words
of reassurance. I wondered if I was the only person who
wasn't scandalized over what I had decided to do.

Through the fog of sedatives coming through my IV
back in the present, I see my gynecologist smiling at me
from the end of the table. I'm so accustomed to seeing him
in his homey suburban office—all the nice pregnant ladies
toting around their urine-filled Dixie cups, the Pap smear
parade of middle-agers like myself. This place, what I think
goes on here, seems so unlikely for him. It is probably the
drugs, but before I can stop myself, I blurt out, "Are you
doing abortions here?"

The OR falls dead silent. My doctor's eyes dart over
to the masked nurse next to him. Another second of utter
quiet. I can hear her clear her throat before she calmly
replies, "Yes. We do abortions here, among other things.
Do you have a problem with that?" I realize they probably
think I'm going to return to the clinic with a sandwich
sign, or worse. "No, of course not! I had an abortion in
my twenties," I babble in my drugged-out attempt to put
everyone at ease. I'm sure they are as grateful as I am that

the drugs knock me out before I can make the scene any more insane.

It takes four full days for the anesthesia to leave my body. And six days more before Paul and I can make love again. Only four times in my life has the anticipation and excitement about sex compared to this moment: the night I lost my virginity, the first time Paul and I made love, and each first unprotected attempt to conceive our two children. I come to bed and stand statue-still in front of it. Here I am, I marvel. In this house, in this life, with this *man*. All is what it has been, but I am different. I reach for my husband and set myself free.

Contributors

SHAUN ASSAEL is the author of the *New York Times* best seller *Sex, Lies, and Headlocks: The Real Story of Vince McMahon* and of a forthcoming history of steroids in America. He lives in suburban New York with his wife and son.

ERIC BARTELS is a feature writer for the *Portland Tribune* newspaper in Portland, Oregon, where he lives with his wife and two children. His essay "My Problem with Her Anger" appeared in the collection *The Bastard on the Couch*.

PATRICIA BERRY is a freelance writer and a founding editor of *Sports Illustrated for Kids*. Her work has appeared in *This Old House*, the *New York Times*, *Working Mother*, *Fortune Small Business*, and *New Jersey Monthly*. She has served as an editorial consultant for ClubMom.com and for *Money Magazine's Money for Teens*. She lives in New Jersey with her husband and three daughters.

ANNE BURT is the editor of the essay collection *My Father Married Your Mother: Dispatches from the Blended Family*. Her essays and fiction have appeared on NPR's *All Things Considered* and *Talk of the Nation*, and in publications including *Salon*, the *Christian Science Monitor*, *Parenting*, and *Working Mother*. She won *Meridian* literary magazine's 2002 Editors' Prize in Fiction. She lives in New Jersey with her husband, daughter, and stepdaughter.

DEBORAH CALDWELL is the managing editor of Beliefnet (www.beliefnet.com) and an award-winning writer on the subject of religion and politics. She was one of the primary editors of *Taking Back Islam*, which won a Wilbur Award for best religion book of the year, and *The Beliefnet Guide to Islam*. Her writing has appeared in the *New York Times* "Week in Review" and *Slate*, along with the collections *Perspectives on the Passion of the Christ* and *The Imperfect Mother: Candid Confessions of Mothers Living in the Real World*. She lives in New Jersey with her two children.

SUSAN CHEEVER is the author of twelve books, including five novels and a biography of Alcoholics Anonymous co-founder Bill Wilson. Her latest book, *American Bloomsbury*, is a group biography of Henry David Thoreau, Nathaniel Hawthorne, Margaret Fuller, Ralph Waldo Emerson, and Louisa May Alcott. She teaches in the Bennington College writing seminars and at the New School, and lives in New York City.

MICHAEL CORCORAN is the deputy editor of *Golf* magazine and the author of eight books, including *The Game of the Century, For Which It Stands,* and *Duel in the Sun.* He has written for such publications as *The Scotsman, Scotland on Sunday, Philadelphia* magazine, *Outside, Men's Health,* and *Golf* magazine. Corcoran was an editor at the humor-slanted *Stuff* magazine, as well as at *Men's Health, Golf Illustrated,* and *Golf Digest.* He lives in New York and Pennsylvania with his wife and their three children.

SUSAN CRANDELL is the author of *Thinking about Tomorrow: Reinventing Yourself at Midlife* and the former editor in chief of *More* magazine. She has written for such magazines as *Town & Country, Luxury SpaFinder, AARP, More, Travel and Leisure, Prevention, Ladies' Home Journal, Gourmet, Reader's Digest,* and *Country Home.* She lives in upstate New York with her husband, writer Stephan Wilkinson.

ALICE ELLIOTT DARK is the author of the novel *Think of England* and two collections of short stories, *In the Gloaming* and *Naked to the Waist*. Her work has appeared in *The New Yorker*, *Harper's*, *Redbook*, *DoubleTake*, *Best American Short Stories*, *Prize Stories: The O. Henry Awards*, *Best American Short Stories of the Century*, and has been translated into many languages. Her story "In the Gloaming" was made into films by HBO and Trinity Playhouse. Her nonfiction has appeared in the *New York Times*, the *Washington Post*, and various anthologies. She is a past recipient of a National Endowment for the Arts fellowship, and lives in New Jersey with her husband and son.

LIAN DOLAN is the cohost of the nationally syndicated radio show *Satellite Sisters* and the senior editor of their book *Satellite Sisters' Uncommon Senses*. She writes a monthly column in *Working Mother* magazine, called "The Chaos Chronicles," and has written for such magazines as *O: The Oprah Magazine* and *Good Housekeeping*. She lives in California with her husband and two children.

MAREK FUCHS is a writer for the *New York Times*, providing backup coverage of the New York Knicks and contributing regularly to many of the newspaper's other sections. He writes the "Business Press Maven" column for TheStreet.com. Fuchs lives in suburban New York with his wife and three children.

ANN HOOD is the best-selling author of ten books, including the novels *The Knitting Circle*, *Somewhere Off the Coast of Maine*, and *Ruby*; a memoir, *Do Not Go Gentle: My Search for Miracles in a Cynical Time*; and a short-story collection, *An Ornithologist's Guide to Life*. Her short stories and essays have appeared in the *New York Times*, *Glimmer Train*, *Double Take*, the *Missouri Review*, the *Washington Post*, *Traveler*, *Bon Appétit*, and many other publications. She has won a Best American Spiritual Writing Award, a Pushcart Prize, and the Paul Bowles Prize for Short Fiction. She lives in Rhode Island with her husband and two children.

ADAIR LARA, columnist, author, and magazine writer, is the author of a memoir about her teenage daughter, *Hold Me Close, Let Me Go,* and the founder of a new Web site for meeting other writers, Matchwriters.com.

CAROLINE LEAVITT is the author of eight novels, most recently *Girls in Trouble*. The recipient of a New York Foundation of the Arts Award, a National Magazine Award nominee, and a Nickelodeon screenwriting fellowship finalist, she most recently won a Goldenberg literary honorable mention prize for portions of her novel in progress. She is the former book columnist for the *Boston Globe*. Leavitt lives in New Jersey with her husband, writer Jeff Tamarkin, and their son.

SARAH MAHONEY is a contributing editor for *Parents* and *Prevention*. Her work has appeared in such national publications as *Woman's Day, Better Homes and Gardens, Reader's Digest,* and the *New York Times.* She was editor of *Ladies' Home Journal,* editor in chief of *Fitness* magazine, and executive editor of *Parents* magazine. She lives in Maine with her husband and two children.

JOYCE MAYNARD has worked as a reporter with the *New York Times,* a syndicated columnist, a magazine journalist, a commentator on National Public Radio's *All Things Considered,* and a novelist. Her novel *To Die For* was adapted into a film directed by Gus Van Sant and starring Nicole Kidman. She has published two volumes of memoirs, including the best-selling *At Home in the World,* translated into nine languages. Her five novels include *The Usual Rules,* named one of the ten best young-adult books of 2003. Maynard's latest book is *Internal Combustion: The True Story of a Marriage and a Murder in Motor City.* A longtime teacher of writing, she runs the Lake Atitlan Writing Workshop in Guatemala, as well as workshops in her home.

KATE MEYERS is a freelance writer whose work has appeared in *Life, InStyle, Sports Illustrated, Golf, Golf Digest,* and *Golf for Women.* She was an editor at *Travel and Leisure Golf* and a staff writer at *Entertainment Weekly.* Meyers lives in Colorado with her two daughters.

JACQUELYN MITCHARD is the author of the number one *New York Times* best-selling novel *The Deep End of the Ocean*—chosen as the first book for Oprah Winfrey's Book Club—and five other novels: *The Most Wanted; A Theory of Relativity; Twelve Times Blessed; Christmas, Present;* and, most recently, *The Breakdown Lane.* She also is the author of an essay collection, *The Rest of Us: Dispatches from the Mothership,* and five books for children and young adults. Her syndicated column appears in 128 newspapers nationwide, and she is a contributing editor for *Parenting* and *Wondertime.* Mitchard lives in Wisconsin with her husband and their six children.

STEVEN RINEHART is the author of the story collection *Kick in the Head* and the novel *Built in a Day.* His stories have been published in a variety of magazines, including *Harper's, GQ, Story,* and *Ploughshares.* He is the recipient of both NEA and Michener fellowships. Rinehart lives in New York City with his wife and three children.

PEG ROSEN has written about love, health, parenting, and family for such publications as *Cosmopolitan, Self, Redbook, Ladies' Home Journal, Parents, Good Housekeeping,* and *American Baby.* A former editor at *Brides* and *Child,* she is the coauthor, with Vicki Iovine, of *Girlfriends' Guide to Baby Gear* and *Girlfriends' Guide to Parties and Playdates.* She lives in New Jersey with her husband and two sons.

CRISPIN SARTWELL is associate professor of political science at Dickinson College. His commentaries on popular culture, politics, education, and religion have appeared in the *Philadelphia Inquirer*, the *Los Angeles Times*, the *Baltimore Sun*, and the *Washington Post*. His weekly op-ed columns are syndicated by Creators, and his essays have appeared in *Harper's* and on National Public Radio. Sartwell has published a number of books with university presses, including *Six Names of Beauty* and *Extreme Virtue: Leadership and Truth in Five Great American Lives*. He lives in Pennsylvania with his wife, the writer Marion Winik, and their five children.

HELENE STAPINSKI is the author of the best-selling memoir *Five-Finger Discount: A Crooked Family History* and *Baby Plays Around: A Love Affair, with Music*. She has written for the *New York Times*, *New York* magazine, *Billboard*, *Columbia Journalism Review*, *Salon*, *Real Simple*, *Food & Wine*, and many other magazines and newspapers. She lives in Brooklyn with her husband and their two small children.

CAMERON STRACHER is the author of a memoir, *Double Billing: A Young Lawyer's Tale of Greed, Sex, Lies, and the Pursuit of a Swivel Chair*, and a novel, *The Laws of Return*, for which he won a fiction fellowship from the New York Foundation for the Arts. A graduate of Harvard Law School and the Iowa Writers' Workshop, he is the publisher of the *New York Law School Law Review*. He lives in Connecticut with his wife and two children.

JOSEPHINE THOMAS is the pseudonym of a freelance writer whose work has appeared in *Health, Self, Redbook, Marie Claire, Parents,* and *Parenting.* She lives in New Jersey with her husband and two children.

STEPHAN WILKINSON is the automotive correspondent of *Condé Nast Traveler* magazine, consulting auto editor of *Popular Science,* and a frequent contributor to *Golf Connoisseur* and Forbesautos.com. He also is the author of *Man and Machine: The Best of Stephan Wilkinson* and the memoir *The Gold-Plated Porsche: How I Sank a Small Fortune into a Used Car, and Other Misadventures.* He lives in upstate New York with his wife, writer Susan Crandell.

MARION WINIK, a commentator on National Public Radio's *All Things Considered* since 1991, is the author of *Above Us Only Sky; Telling; First Comes Love;* and *The Lunch-Box Chronicles,* among others. Her articles and essays have appeared in such magazines as *O: The Oprah Magazine, Salon, Travel and Leisure, National Geographic Traveler, Texas Monthly, Men's Journal, Reader's Digest,* and *Redbook,* along with many newspapers, Web sites, and anthologies. She lives in Pennsylvania with her husband, Crispin Sartwell, and their five children.

Acknowledgments

I am so grateful to the many people who encouraged me to do this book—and stayed on me until I did. Chief among them: Naomi Rand, for her patience and gentle guidance; Candy Cooper, for keeping me honest and motivated; Pat Berry and Peg Rosen, for giving without thinking twice; Anne Burt, for generously bailing me out; and Alice Elliott Dark, for her instant and enduring enthusiasm. Also, the women in Writers Group, whose support, solace, friendship, and advice have helped make this a safe and happy journey.

A special thanks to Jacquelyn Mitchard, Marion Winik, Kate Meyers, and Cameron Stracher for offering up their incredible talent with no guarantees, and to all the contributors who shared their most personal and poignant experiences so we could all ride the ups and downs of middle age together.

My agent, Nina Collins, and editor, Michelle Howry, took this idea, sharpened and shaped it, and turned it into reality. Without them, these stories would not have been told.